UNDERSTANDING THE

BIBLE

The Gift Of Free Will

Bruno Marian

ISBN: 979-8-90252-040-5   (Paperback)
ISBN: 979-8-90252-041-2   (eBook)

Printed in the United States of America

God destroyed the world, about 1700 years after Adam and Eve, with the great flood, because people were not living the way God wanted them to live. With the exception of Noah and his family and the animals on the ark, God allowed for humans to start over, giving them a chance to live the way God wanted them to live. God promised He would never again destroy the world with a flood, and wanted humans to live the way He wanted them to live.

For about 2400 years, humans, ALL humans lived again, the way they wanted to live, and God sent His son, Jesus, in human form to "correct" the way that humans, all humans were living. Jesus was sent for 3 very important reasons, to teach humans how God wanted them to live, to start a new religion, and to forgive the sins of the world, the whole world.

It is written in the scriptures, by humans, that the tribes of Israel are "God's chosen people", but in reality, God does not discriminate and ALL people, yes ALL people were created by GOD! God loves all people, God cares for all people, God wants all people to love Him. God will judge ALL people when we die and our soul leaves our dead human body and goes before Jesus for final judgment, ALL PEOPLE!

The BIG question that people need to ask is this: IF all people were living the way God wanted them to live, why did Jesus have to teach the people, all people how God wanted them to live? If the religion that people were practicing was what God wanted, why did Jesus start a new religion, Christianity? If people, all people were living the way God wanted them to live, why did Jesus have to forgive the SINS of the world by shedding his blood on the cross, one sacrifice for all, to forgive the sins of the whole world?

I'm sure that the above statements will cause some people to say that I am against certain people, when that would NOT BE TRUE! This is not anti anything, it is PRO GOD, PRO JESUS, and the only way we, as humans, can heave eternity with God, is to make sure that our FREE WILL choices are aligned with the way that GOD wants all humans to live.

Jesus, (God in human form), taught, the lust of money can be the root of all evil, and He also taught people should live by need and not by want, and love your neighbor as yourself. It's been 2,000 years since Jesus was on earth in human form, and the question for all of us should be, when will humans start to live the way God has always wanted humans to live. Our eternity depends on how we choose to use the gift of FREE WILL that God gave to ALL OF US at conception?

Jesus also taught that when God breathed life into each and every one of us at conception, He also gave each of us a Soul, our spiritual self, and when we die, and all of us will die, our soul will leave our dead human body and go face to face with Jesus for final judgment. We will ALL be judged by how we have used the gift of Free Will that God also gave each of us at conception, and the choices we have made while on this earth. Even though we, humans, think we can get by with stealing, cheating, and how we treat others, GOD already knows, and each of us will have to answer for what we have done at final judgment, God knows the beginning and the end and everything all of us have done while alive on this earth, and we will be judged for what we have done for eternity. What humans don't realize, is that no matter what we have done, we cannot lie to God, because God already knows the truth! Jesus also taught this, "To enter life, (eternity with God), we must enter by the narrow gate and few will find it, for the wide gate leads to destruction". What that means is that there is a stairway to heaven, but it will not be crowded, and there is a super highway to Hell, and a ton of people vying for pole position on that super highway to Hell! GOD, Jesus, will judge each of us on how we used our gift of free will, and we will not be able to lie to Jesus on judgment day.

Remember, when we die, and all of us will die, we will not be able to take so much as one penny with us when we die. Our human body will be put into a box and face corruption, turn back to dust, but our soul will leave our dead human body and go face to face with Jesus for final judgment!

AGAIN, this is NOT anti anybody, any group, or any country, this is PRO GOD, PRO JESUS, and above all it is understanding God, understanding Jesus, and UNDERSTANDING THE BIBLE!

TABLE OF CONTENTS

DEDICATION

This book is dedicated to the memory of Charlie Kirk, whose words and witness reminded so many of the gift God has given us: free will.

Though I did not know Charlie while writing these pages, I later discovered how closely his message echoed the very heart of what is written here: that each of us has the freedom to choose how we will live, yet every choice carries eternal weight.

Charlie spoke with conviction about faith, responsibility, and truth. His life reflected love for God, family, country, and neighbor. In honoring his memory, I also honor the God who gives each of us the ability to believe, to follow, and to serve.

As Scripture tells us, "Choose this day whom you will serve" (Joshua 24:15). Charlie's life was a testimony to that choice. May this book continue that message and encourage all who read it to see the Bible not only as God's Word but also as the mirror that reveals how we are living in response to Him.

God bless Charlie, his family, and all who walk in the truth he stood for.

Bruno Marian

PRELUDE

For years, I made a habit of reading the Bible, but the more I read, the more frustrated I became. I pressed on and read it from cover to cover, yet the frustration did not go away.

Hoping a different translation might help, I turned to one version after another: King James Version (KJV), New International Version (NIV), English Standard Version (ESV), New American Standard Bible (NASB), and the Revised Standard Version (RSV).

But no matter which version I read, the same question unsettled me: how can so many people in the Bible be called highly esteemed when they do not live by God's commandments?

For example, David was called a man after God's own heart, yet he committed adultery and murder. God gave Solomon wisdom, yet his many foreign wives led him into idolatry. Peter was a pillar of the early church, yet he denied Jesus three times.

It is also clear that God created the entire universe and everything in and on the earth, including human beings. Likewise, the Bible clearly teaches that God breathes life into every human being at the moment of their conception and gives each person a soul, which is our spiritual self.

We also know from scripture that when we die, all of us will leave our bodies and be face-to-face with Jesus for the final judgment.

But what always puzzled me was the third gift that God gave each of us at conception: the gift of free will.

Yet that is the key to understanding the Bible. But for so many years, I didn't understand what the gift of free will had to do with what is written in the scriptures.

The Bible tells us that the Holy Spirit, the third person of the Godhead, "inspired" the writers of scripture to document God's revelation. But even knowing this, I just could not understand why the scriptures spoke about people who were not abiding by God's word.

While sorting some coins that I collected in a jar to take to the bank, I was looking at a quarter and noticed for the first time that each side had a different engraving on it, and then it made sense. That is what the Holy Spirit inspired the scripture writers to write: BOTH SIDES!

It struck me that a coin always has two sides. You cannot understand its full value unless you see both. In the same way, the Holy Spirit inspired scripture to show us both sides: how God intends us to live and how people actually live. Without seeing both, the story is incomplete.

What is in the Bible is how God wants human beings to live and how human beings actually live – both sides – and that is what free will is all about.

A pastor told me many years ago that God does not lie and God cannot sin. The Bible gives us both sides, and we can choose how we want to live. And when we die, Jesus will judge us according to whether we have lived as God wants humans to live!

When you understand the gift of free will and how the Holy Spirit inspired the scripture writers to include both sides of the story, you will see where we as human beings are, where we should be, and where we are headed for eternity.

I hope this will help you in understanding why I wrote this book, and what a wonderful God we have to assist us in our life's journey!

In the pages that follow, we will walk from Creation to Revelation, tracing how free will has shaped human history and continues to shape our choices today. My hope is that you will see the Bible with new clarity, not only as God's Word, but as the mirror that reveals how we live in response to Him.

Chapter 1

THE GIFT OF GOD

Understanding the Bible is very interesting, to say the least. It was written by the inspiration of the Holy Spirit, which makes it unlike any other book. Even a cursory reading of the 66 canonical books teaches us how God wants human beings to live on the earth that He created.

He gives laws, commandments, statutes, ordinances, and decrees, and He wants all human beings to obey them. God's laws are not difficult to live by if we want to spend eternity with Him in heaven.

Moreover, God's laws are the same; yesterday, today, and tomorrow. They do not change, which makes it simple to follow Him, regardless of how much society changes.

As God says in the Old Testament, "I the Lord do not change" (Malachi 3:6). And Jesus reminds us, "For truly I tell you, until heaven and earth disappear, not the smallest letter, not the least stroke of a pen, will by any means disappear from the Law until everything is accomplished." (Matthew 5:18).

In the Jewish tradition, the smallest letter of the Hebrew alphabet, the *yod*, was considered a symbol of precision. When Jesus said not even the smallest letter or stroke would pass away, He was affirming that every detail of God's Word is ultimate and eternal.

This is the authority of God's Word, but it also means that obedience is not selective. We cannot choose parts of the Bible that are convenient and ignore the rest. God's law is complete, consistent, and enduring.

We live in a world created by God, and He not only created the world and everything in it, but also created human beings in His own image and likeness. He did so because of the love He has for mankind and the desire to share that love with all human beings.

Reading the Bible, we also see the progress that humans have made, and we discover the frustration that God has experienced with how humans have lived in the world that He created.

In that frustration, God destroyed everything in the world with the Great Flood (since the people up to that point were not living up to His standards), with the exception of eight people and the animals on Noah's ark, and let them start over (Genesis 6 - 9).

Did you know that ancient cultures from Mesopotamia to India also record flood traditions? This suggests a common memory of this cataclysm. But while other ancient cultures also had stories about the flood, the Biblical account differs in its moral purpose: the flood was not simply a natural disaster, but a divine response to human wickedness.

Noah's story shows that one person's obedience can preserve a future for humanity. His faith is a reminder that even in times of judgment, God provides a way of salvation for those who listen. That is why Noah is listed as a faithful witness in scripture (Hebrews 11:7).

As time went on and the earth was repopulated, humans again began to live as they wanted, rather than as God wanted them to live.

But God promised never to destroy the earth with a flood again, so he sent His Son, in the form of a man, to show people by His teaching and example how to live the way that God intended. We will learn more about the Great Flood and how it helps us understand the Bible in Chapter 3.

The Mission of Jesus

God's response to human rebellion was not another flood or an act of destruction. Instead, out of love, He sent His Son into the world as an adjustment to the way people were living.

Humanity had once again chosen its own path, and now God decided to intervene in a new and decisive way. Jesus came to accomplish three essential missions, each revealing God's love and purpose for the world.

First, Jesus came to teach. His entire life was a testament to how God intended humans to live. He healed the sick, welcomed children, defended the poor, and forgave those who wronged Him.

He preached the Sermon on the Mount, showing that righteousness is not about outward appearances but about the condition of the heart (Matthew 5–7).

Jesus taught in parables, using simple stories to reveal eternal truths. His life and words together gave humanity a living picture of obedience to the Father's will.

Second, Jesus came to establish a new covenant and begin the movement we now call "Christianity."

From the beginning, He called disciples to follow Him. He chose twelve apostles, trained them, and sent them out to preach the good news. He gave them authority to heal, cast out demons, and announce that the kingdom of God was near (Luke 9:1–2).

Before His death, He promised that the Holy Spirit would come to guide them into all truth (John 16:13). What began as a small group of fishermen and tax collectors would grow into a worldwide church, carrying the message of salvation to every nation.

Third, Jesus came to forgive the sins of the world by His death on the cross. By doing so, He fulfilled the sacrifices of the Old Testament. Those sacrifices were temporary and repeated daily, but Jesus' sacrifice on the cross was once for all. As Hebrews 10:10 declares, "We have been made holy through the sacrifice of the body of Jesus Christ once for all."

By shedding His blood, He opened the way for reconciliation between God and humanity. His death was not a tragic accident but the central act of God's plan to redeem His people.

The story does not end with the cross. After He rose from the dead, Jesus spent forty days with His disciples, proving that He was alive and restoring their courage (Acts 1:3).

The disciples had scattered in fear when He was crucified, but He gathered them again, strengthened their faith, and gave them the Great Commission: "Go and make disciples of all nations" (Matthew 28:19).

It was during these forty days after his resurrection that Jesus secured the future of His church, ensuring that His mission would continue until the end of time.

Through these three missions — teaching, establishing His church, and giving His life for the world — Jesus fulfilled God's purpose in a way that no prophet or law could. He not only revealed how we are meant to live but also gave us the power and the Spirit to live it out.

This is why His coming is the turning point of history and the greatest expression of God's gift of free will. Humanity had chosen disobedience again and again, but in Christ, God provided both the example and the salvation we need to choose His way.

Jesus, the Perfect Sacrifice

As mentioned above, Jesus performed His mission with love, care, healing, and teaching.

However, human beings were offended by Jesus' teachings because they opposed the way they wanted to live. This led to the crucifixion of Jesus, where he shed his blood for the forgiveness of all our sins.

You see, God also wanted to forgive the many, many sins of humans, and to do so, there needed to be "one sacrifice for all," instead of the animal sacrifices that people did in hopes of receiving forgiveness.

Humans were sacrificing countless animals, thinking that the blood of these creatures would forgive their sins. But God sent Jesus to shed his blood to forgive the sins of humans, one sacrifice for all people.

As you read this book, you will see what Jesus did and why he did what he did. However, humans still live the way they want to live and not the way God wants, even after 2000 years since Jesus walked this earth.

What Defiles a Person?

When Jesus was on this earth, he demonstrated this exact issue when he told his apostles that what goes in the mouth does not defile a person, because it goes into the body and is used up, and what is left goes in the sewer. It is what comes out of the mouth that defiles a person, as what comes out of the mouth comes from the heart.

Jesus told this to his apostles because the Pharisees were complaining that the apostles did not wash their hands before they ate, and taught that handling food with unwashed hands would defile a person (Mark 7:5). This is an example of how God wants humans to live vs. how humans actually live.

But Jesus taught that if the heart is right with God, what comes out of the mouth is good and just. But if the heart of a person is not right, what comes out of the mouth will defile that person (Mark 7:15).

The Leaven of the Pharisees

Another example is when Jesus told the apostles to beware of the leaven of the Pharisees and the Sadducees (Matthew 16:6).

The apostles thought Jesus was saying this because they did not bring any bread with them (Matthew 16:7). Jesus was actually telling them to beware of what the Pharisees and the Sadducees were teaching the masses, because it is contrary to Christ's teachings, i.e., how God wants people to live.

Let the Children Come to Me

The third example (and there are many) is when Jesus told his apostles to let the young people come to Him, rather than trying to keep them away.

He said, "let the little children come to me and do not hinder them, for to such as these belongs the Kingdom of heaven." (Matthew 19:14). What Jesus was telling the apostles was that young children have not yet been taught the ways of adults, which, once again, are diametrically opposed to God's moral code for our lives.

Children were considered inferior in the ancient world. But the Bible uses the word "children" as an illustration of faith and obedience.

You see, children exemplify trust, dependence, and openness. By pointing to them, Jesus was reminding His disciples that the kingdom is not earned through status or achievement, but is received with humility.

In the Roman world, children had little social standing. By lifting them up as models, Jesus was turning the values of His society upside down, and He continues to challenge our social and cultural norms and assumptions as well.

Free Will - The Gift of God

Jesus showed that the way people had been taught to live was not what God intended. The Holy Spirit inspired scripture to reveal both sides: God's design for life and humanity's reality. Much of what Jesus taught stood in sharp contrast to how people were actually living, so he called his followers to a different way.

The four gospels, though told from different perspectives, agree on this truth. Their variations reflect the writers' memories, yet all emphasize how Jesus lived and what he taught. Different Bible translations may use different wording, but the message remains: Scripture records both God's will and human choices.

Understanding this makes it clear why God gave humanity free will. The Bible shows the contrast between divine intention and human action, so we can see that each of us has the choice of how to live in God's world.

If you want to see how we live, just observe the people around you. The speed limit on the freeway is 70 mph, but many of us drive at 80 or 90 mph.

People also park in handicapped spaces illegally because they are in a hurry and don't want to walk to their destination.

The best (actually the worst) example of how we live is our addiction to the phone. People can't shop without being on their phones, and even while shopping, the phone is still in their hands.

Shopping itself has shifted to the internet, where people scroll, buy, and then wait for packages to arrive. At pro sports games, despite the high price of tickets, the cameras reveal crowds staring at their phones. At concerts, the same thing happens; people watch their screens more than the performance they paid to see.

Likewise, at church, instead of listening to the sermon, many are texting. We stay so busy with our devices that we leave little time for anything, least of all for God.

The danger of distraction is not new. Augustine of Hippo, writing in the fourth century, confessed that he too was "scattered in times and places" by worldly pleasures before he turned fully to God.

Our modern distractions, whether technology, entertainment, or consumerism, are simply new forms of the same human restlessness. The core question remains: what holds our attention most, God or the world?

Another thing that people don't understand, or don't want to understand, is this: God does not lie, and He cannot sin (Titus 1:2, Hebrews 16:8, and James 1:13). I have stated this before and will say it again.

So why would a loving, caring, merciful, and forgiving God give us the gift of free will, the ability to choose, if he didn't want us to *choose* to follow Him instead of our own ways?

That is why God had to be disappointed with us as he was with our ancestors before the Great Flood, and even those who survived and lived till the time of Jesus Christ.

I know that Jesus will judge us when we die, just as he did those who have passed before us, all the way back to creation.

All the way from the beginning to our present day, God has acted with the highest integrity, and we can believe that God will not change what He promised to do for us, and that is to love us, care for us, have mercy on us, and forgive us when we reconcile with Him.

Even though humans do not have the character to love and trust God, we can be assured that God does not lie and God cannot sin.

Understanding the Bible

When we read the Bible, we need open minds to see how the Holy Spirit inspired the writers to show both sides: how God wants us to live and how we often choose to live.

Understanding how the Bible was written helps us make better choices in this life, choices that shape where we will spend eternity. Judgment is certain, and no one escapes it. With that in mind, the wise decision is to live as God calls us to live.

About 1,700 years after creation, God sent the flood to correct human rebellion. Around 2,400 years later, Jesus came, teaching again how God wants us to live. Now, about 2,000 years after Jesus, humanity has drifted even farther away. Technology and innovation have advanced, but they've pulled us deeper into self-centered living and farther from God. Is it unreasonable to think God may soon decide to act again?

In church, we are told the Bible is the word of God, fully true. That remains certain. The Spirit inspired its writers to reveal both God's way and humanity's way. Jesus taught this distinction to his apostles, and the scriptures still clearly demonstrate it.

In the Old Testament, people followed their own desires and made laws that benefited some while oppressing others. The same was true in Jesus' time, and it is still true now. Reading the Bible with this in mind shows just how far we have strayed.

Two thousand years after Christ, modern life leaves even less room for God. Church is often squeezed in, if at all, around entertainment, shopping, and social plans. If we continue living this way, how long before God decides He no longer has time for us? How long before He chooses to act again?

The Bible is one of the most important books ever published, and a very educational book to read. The Bible provides us with a history that allows us to trace and understand how God created the world we inhabit, what He expects from human beings, and how to live in the world He created for all humans.

It also demonstrates the power and love of God, as He created a world for humans to share in His love, mercy, grace, understanding, and forgiveness. It also gives us a chance to understand, to some extent, the power of God, along with how God loves all human beings. God created the earth, the solar system, the galaxies, and the universe, which is very hard to really understand as a human being with our minimal capabilities.

As we read the Bible, we learn that there are three persons in one Godhead: the Father, the Son, and the Holy Spirit. All three work together for the good of creation and mankind.

Till now, we have seen that from the very beginning, God's laws have remained the same while human choices have wavered. The rest of this book will explore what those choices look like across history and what they mean for us today. But it all begins at the moment of creation.

Chapter 2

GOD'S BEAUTIFUL CREATION

God created the entire universe, which shows His greatness and vision (Genesis 1:1; Psalm 19:1). God also made the atmosphere, which varies with the seasons (Genesis 8:22), and the sun to warm the earth during the day (Genesis 1:16; Psalm 136:8).

He created the moon to give light and guidance during the night (Genesis 1:16; Psalm 104:19). The daylight is for people to do what they need to do (John 9:4), and the night is for people to rest after a hard day's work (Psalm 104:23).

He also created the earth with all its intricate details (Isaiah 45:18), a wonderful place for human beings to live! God created all the plants in the Garden, including the trees that provide shade, and they produced fruit for humans to eat (Genesis 1:29; Genesis 2:9).

God also created the birds, animals, and even things that crawled on the ground (Genesis 1:20–25). God did all of this for the humans He created to live in the beautiful garden (Genesis 2:8).

Each stage of creation in Genesis ends with the refrain, "And God saw that it was good." This repeated affirmation suggests that the world is not random or chaotic, but rather purposeful.

The Science of Creation

When we look at the natural world, we see order and design that point to God's wisdom. The creation account in Genesis describes light, water, sky, land, plants, and animals, all arranged in perfect sequence.

Today, scientists have discovered layers of precision behind these words. The Earth sits at just the proper distance from the Sun. If it were closer, life would burn; if it were further, life would freeze. Our planet tilts on its axis at just the right angle to give us seasons, and the moon keeps our tides in balance. Even the air we breathe, a blend of oxygen and nitrogen, is ideally suited for life.

Modern physics calls this "fine-tuning." It means that if even one constant in the universe (the pull of gravity, the speed of light, or the strength of the atom) were slightly altered, life could not exist.

Some call this a coincidence. Others say it is a chance. But the Bible teaches that "God is not a God of disorder but of peace" (1 Corinthians 14:33). The order in creation reflects the God who planned it.

This has everything to do with free will. God could have made a barren world where humans were forced to survive by instinct alone. Instead, He created a world rich with beauty and balance, where we have the freedom to explore, to build, to discover, and to choose.

In contrast, the theory of evolution teaches that life appeared by accident and then slowly changed over millions of years. According to this idea, people are not here because of God's purpose but because of chance and survival.

If this is true, then human life has no special meaning. We would be just another animal, guided by instinct and competition. Right and wrong would not be fixed; they would only be what helps the strongest survive.

History has shown how dangerous this way of thinking can be. When people believed that life was only about the survival of the fittest, it became easier to mistreat others.

In the last century, some leaders used evolutionary ideas to claim that certain races were superior to others, or that the weak and disabled should be removed from society. This led to policies of oppression, injustice, and even mass killings. When life is explained only by chance, human dignity is quickly forgotten.

The Bible tells us something very different. Every person is created in the image of God. This means every life has value, from the strongest to the weakest.

Our choices are not just survival instincts. They are the decisions of souls made by God and for God. This is why free will is such a precious gift. It shows that we are more than accidents of nature. We were made with purpose, and every choice we make has eternal meaning. I will write more about this in the coming chapters.

For now, it is sufficient to know that the Bible presents the facts of creation, whereas evolution is a fairy tale, not science.

In fact, every scientific breakthrough that uncovers more of the universe's secrets only deepens the wonder: the God who fine-tuned the stars also fine-tuned our lives, giving us freedom to live in harmony with Him or apart from Him.

Modern science has revealed extraordinary order in the universe, from the fine-tuning of physical constants to the complex balance of ecosystems. For believers, this order points not to accident but to design, which reflects the wisdom of the Creator.

So, why did God create man and woman if He is such a supreme being who can do everything? The answer is very simple: He wanted to share His love with human beings, and He created them in His own image and likeness out of love (Genesis 1:26–27; 1 John 4:8).

The Image of God (Imago Dei)

The creation account climaxes not with the sun or stars, but with humanity: "So God created mankind in his own image, in the image of God he created them; male and female he created them" (Genesis 1:27). Being made in the *Imago Dei* sets humans apart from every other creature. Animals may be strong, fast, or clever, but only humans carry God's likeness.

What does this mean? To bear God's image is to be capable of a relationship with Him. It means we can think, feel, choose, and love in ways that mirror God's character. When we show compassion, we reflect His mercy. When we create beauty, we echo His creativity. When we choose justice, we walk in His righteousness.

But the image also gives weight to our choices. If we were mere animals, bound by instinct, disobedience would mean little. But because we bear God's image, every act of love or selfishness, forgiveness or hatred, obedience or rebellion has eternal significance. To misuse free will is to distort the image of God within us.

Throughout Scripture, God plans to restore this image. Paul writes that believers are being "conformed to the image of his Son" (Romans 8:29). Jesus is described as "the image of the invisible God" (Colossians 1:15). The story of salvation is not just about escaping judgment; it is about becoming what we were created to be: living mirrors of God's glory.

Early church fathers such as Irenaeus described humanity as "capable of God," which is being able to know Him and reflect His glory. This high calling explains why sin is so tragic: it distorts the very image we were meant to bear.

Agape (God's Unconditional Love)

God's love is not only a feeling but the very foundation of His relationship with humanity. From the beginning, love shaped every part of creation. The prophet Jeremiah records God's words: "I have loved you with an everlasting love; I have drawn you with unfailing kindness" (Jeremiah 31:3).

This everlasting love is the same love that moved Him to breathe life into Adam and Eve and place them in a garden of abundance. Every tree that was pleasant to the eye and good for food was a reminder that God's love provides before we even ask.

The greatest proof of God's love is that He gives Himself to us. John 3:16 tells us that "God so loved the world that he gave his one and only Son."

If His love was seen in creation, it is seen even more in redemption. He did not abandon humanity when it turned away from His design.

Instead, His love pursued us, first through covenants and prophets, and finally through Christ. This shows that His love is not dependent on our goodness but flows from His own character.

God's love also establishes the worth of every human being. Because He loved Adam and Eve, He called them by name and gave them each other as partners (Genesis 2:19, 22; 3:20).

Because He loved the children they would have, He blessed them with the command to "be fruitful and multiply" (Genesis 1:28). And because He loves us, every person, from the strongest to the weakest, bears His image and carries eternal value.

In a world where people are judged for their success, appearance, or ability, God's love declares that our value is rooted in Him alone.

The New Testament uses a special word to describe God's love: *agape*. Unlike other kinds of love, which may depend on feelings, attraction, or benefit, *agape* is unconditional. It seeks the good of the other, even at personal cost. This is the love with which God created us and the love with which He redeems us. Paul explains, "But God demonstrates his own love (*agape*) for us in this: While we were still sinners, Christ died for us" (Romans 5:8).

This is also why sin is so tragic. When we reject God's love, we are not merely breaking a rule; we are turning away from the very relationship for which we were made. But God's *agape* never stops.

Even when Adam and Eve disobeyed, God clothed them (Genesis 3:21). Even when Israel turned away, He promised to restore them. And even when humanity crucified His Son, His love turned that act into salvation. *Agape* is love that does not quit.

To understand free will, we must first understand love. Love that is forced is not love at all. God wanted humanity to share in His love freely, not by compulsion. This is why He gave us the ability to choose.

In giving us free will, God was not taking a risk but offering a relationship. He did not make puppets to control but children to love. Every choice we make is therefore an opportunity to return His love or to reject it.

To sum up, God is a God of love, and He wants us to share his love with us (Jeremiah 31:3; John 3:16). He gave all human beings three very important gifts.

Three Divine Gifts

The first gift was the breath of life, which He gives all human beings at the moment of conception (Genesis 2:7; Job 33:4; Psalm 139:13–14).

In Hebrew, the word is *ḥayyîm* (חַיִּים), meaning "living" or "being alive." Life in Scripture is never just survival but fullness of being. In Greek, the New Testament often uses *zoē* (ζωή) to describe life, especially the eternal life that comes from God (John 1:4). In Latin, the word is *vita*, from which we get the English word "vital." Every breath we take is a reminder that life is not our own invention but a gift sustained by God Himself.

Job confessed, "The Spirit of God has made me; the breath of the Almighty gives me life" (Job 33:4). It means that life is sacred because it flows directly from God's Spirit, and it is entrusted to us to protect and to cherish.

The second gift that God gave each of us was a soul, our spiritual self (Ecclesiastes 12:7; Matthew 10:28). The Hebrew word *nephesh* (נֶפֶשׁ) describes the inner self, the living essence that makes a person unique. In Greek, the word is *psychē* (ψυχή), which also gives us our modern word "psyche." The Latin term *anima* carries the sense of the animating principle of life.

Unlike animals, humans bear a soul that reaches beyond the material world. Ecclesiastes 3:11 says that God "has set eternity in the human heart." This means our *nephesh* longs for God, our *psychē* yearns for what is eternal, and our *anima* is restless until it rests in Him.

Now, the third gift that God gave to every human being is the "gift of free will," and that one is a little hard to understand because, without knowing what He intends to happen in our lives, it really makes you wonder why He would give people this gift (Deuteronomy 30:19; Joshua 24:15).

In Hebrew thought, this is expressed in the call to *bachar* (בָּחַר), "to choose," as when Joshua told the people, "Choose (*bachar*) for yourselves this day whom you will serve" (Joshua 24:15). The Greek New Testament often uses the word *thelēma* (θέλημα), meaning "will" or "desire," to describe both God's will and human will. The Latin term *liberum arbitrium* (free choice) became the classic Christian phrase for this gift. Free will is mysterious because it allows us to either align our *thelēma* with God's will or to resist Him. It gives dignity to our choices and weight to our actions. Without it, love would be forced; with it, love becomes real.

God had a plan of how He wanted human beings to live (Jeremiah 29:11; Micah 6:8), but as history shows, humans did the exact opposite (Romans 3:23; Isaiah 53:6). God knew what He was doing, but humans have always thought they know better than Him! (Proverbs 14:12).

Lucifer's Fall

The gift of free will is so powerful that even angels were not exempt from its dangers. Scripture hints at the story of Lucifer, a mighty angel who was radiant with light. Ezekiel 28 describes him as "the seal of perfection, full of wisdom and perfect in beauty."

Yet pride entered his heart. Isaiah 14 records his ambition: "I will ascend to the heavens; I will raise my throne above the stars of God... I will make myself like the Most High."

This rebellion turned an angel of light into the adversary we now call Satan. Revelation 12 shows him cast out of heaven, dragging a third of the angels with him.

What caused such a fall? It was the misuse of free will. Lucifer was given glory, beauty, and authority, but instead of worshiping the Creator, he desired the throne for himself. Pride turned freedom into rebellion.

This matters for us because Satan's strategy has not changed. The temptation he whispered in Eden — "you will be like God" — was the same lie he believed himself. Humanity's fall began when Adam and Eve chose to believe that lie rather than God's truth. Lucifer's story warns us that no creature, however exalted, is beyond the reach of pride.

And it points us to the humility of Christ, who, though He was in very nature God, "made himself nothing… becoming obedient to death, even death on a cross" (Philippians 2:6–8). Where Lucifer grasped for power that was not his, Jesus surrendered power that was His. What a contrast! And this contrast shows us the path of true freedom.

The fall of Lucifer teaches that even among the heavenly host, freedom was real and could be misused. His story sets the stage for the temptation in Eden: the same pride that drove him now whispers to humanity, "You will be like God." The rebellion of the devil also explains why God created free will.

Most importantly, free will makes love possible. Without the ability to choose, love would be nothing more than compulsion.

When God created us, He did not want robots; He wanted children who could respond freely to His love. This is why obedience has eternal significance. Every choice, whether to forgive or to hate, to serve or to exploit, to worship or to ignore, is a reflection of how we use the freedom God entrusted to us.

Unfortunately, humans do not always exercise this right. The Bible is a record of God's love, but also of human disobedience. This is what we will explore in the coming chapter.

Chapter 3

THE FIRST CHOICES AND THEIR CONSEQUENCES

The story of Adam and Eve is found in the very first book of the Bible, Genesis. God created Adam, the first man, "from the dust of the ground," and gave him life by breathing into him (Genesis 2:7). Later, God created Eve, the first woman, from Adam's rib so that he would not be alone (Genesis 2:21-22).

The Hebrew word used here, *tsela'*, can mean "rib" but also "side." This helps us see God's design more clearly. Eve was not taken from Adam's head to rule over him, nor from his feet to be trampled by him, but from his side to walk with him as an equal partner.

Together they would share life, responsibility, and fellowship with God. Genesis 2:24 explains, "That is why a man leaves his father and mother and is united to his wife, and they become one flesh."

The very creation of woman shows that marriage was intended to be a bond of unity and mutual respect. This is an important truth because in many cultures, women were treated as inferior, but the Bible's story of creation honors them from the very beginning.

Together, the man and the woman were placed in a garden called Eden, a paradise filled with trees, rivers, and every kind of fruit.

In the middle of this garden, God planted two special trees: the tree of life and the tree of the knowledge of good and evil (Genesis 2:9). Adam and Eve were free to eat from any tree except one.

God commanded them, "You must not eat from the tree of the knowledge of good and evil, for when you eat from it you will certainly die" (Genesis 2:17). This was not a cruel restriction but a way of giving them a real choice. For love and obedience to be genuine, there must be freedom to choose otherwise.

The Bible tells us that a serpent, described later as Satan or the devil (Revelation 12:9), came into the garden. The serpent tempted Eve by questioning God's word.

He said, "You will not certainly die… For God knows that when you eat from it your eyes will be opened, and you will be like God" (Genesis 3:4-5). Eve listened, saw that the fruit was attractive, and ate it. She also gave some to Adam, and he ate as well (Genesis 3:6).

At once, they realized that they were naked and tried to cover themselves with fig leaves. When God came to them, they hid in fear.

God asked them, "Have you eaten from the tree that I commanded you not to eat from?" (Genesis 3:11). Instead of confessing honestly, Adam blamed Eve, and Eve blamed the serpent (Genesis 3:12-13).

Their first choice was disobedience, and their second choice was dishonesty. Free will had allowed them to trust and obey God, but they chose to go their own way.

Even here, God's mercy was evident. He pronounced the consequences of their actions — pain, toil, and separation from Eden (Genesis 3:16-19) — yet before sending them out, He clothed them with garments of skin (Genesis 3:21).

This simple act showed His care. They could not undo their decision, but God continued to provide for them. Free will had serious consequences, but God's love was not withdrawn.

Life Outside the Garden

After Adam and Eve disobeyed God in the garden, the Bible explains that their lives changed completely. What had once been a place of joy and ease now became a place of struggle. God told them what their choices would mean for the future.

To Eve, He said that childbirth would now be painful and that harmony between husband and wife would be disturbed (Genesis 3:16).

To Adam, He said that the ground itself would be cursed and that food would come only through hard work: "By the sweat of your brow you will eat your food until you return to the ground" (Genesis 3:19).

These were not arbitrary punishments but consequences. Sin had disrupted the perfect order God had made, and now life would bear the weight of that disruption.

Yet, even in the middle of these consequences, God's care is evident. Genesis 3:21 tells us, "The Lord God made garments of skin for Adam and his wife and clothed them."

This small detail shows that although Adam and Eve had failed, God still loved them enough to cover their shame and prepare them for life outside Eden. Instead of abandoning them, He equipped them to live in the new reality their choices had created.

Genesis also emphasizes that Adam and Eve's role was not finished. God had commanded them earlier, "Be fruitful and increase in number; fill the earth and subdue it" (Genesis 1:28).

Even outside the garden, this calling remained. Their family line would continue, and humanity would grow. In other words, free will was still in their hands. They could no longer walk with God in Eden, but they could still choose how to live in the world beyond.

This truth is important for us as well. The Bible says in Romans 3:23 that "all have sinned and fall short of the glory of God."

Like Adam and Eve, we cannot undo wrong choices once they are made. But the story shows that God does not remove our freedom when we fail. Instead, He calls us to use our freedom wisely in the present. Life outside the garden is harder, but it is not without hope. God still provides, and He still calls us to live responsibly in His world.

Cain and Abel

The first children of Adam and Eve were two sons named Cain and Abel. Genesis tells us that Cain worked the soil as a farmer, while Abel kept flocks as a shepherd (Genesis 4:2). In time, both brothers brought offerings to God. Cain offered some of the fruits of the ground, while Abel brought the firstborn of his flock and their fat portions (Genesis 4:3–4). God looked with favor on Abel's offering but did not accept Cain's.

The Bible does not give every detail about why God accepted Abel's sacrifice and not Cain's, but Hebrews 11:4 explains that Abel's offering was given in faith. Abel brought the best of what he had, trusting God fully. Cain, on the other hand, seems to have given without the same devotion of heart. This teaches us that God looks not only at what we give but also at the attitude with which we give it.

Cain's reaction shows the power of free will in human choices. Genesis 4:5 says, "Cain was very angry, and his face was downcast." God spoke directly to him with a warning: "Why are you angry? Why is your face downcast? If you do what is right, will you not be accepted? But if you do not do what is right, sin is crouching at your door; it desires to have you, but you must rule over it" (Genesis 4:6-7). God was telling Cain that he still had a choice. He could master his anger or let it master him.

Sadly, Cain chose the path of violence. He lured Abel into the field and killed him (Genesis 4:8). This was the first murder recorded in the Bible. When God asked Cain where his brother was, Cain replied with a lie: "I don't know. Am I my brother's keeper?" (Genesis 4:9). Just as Adam and Eve had chosen to deny responsibility in the garden, Cain chose to deny his responsibility for Abel's life.

God's judgment was severe but not without mercy. He told Cain that Abel's blood cried out from the ground (Genesis 4:10) and that Cain would now be a restless wanderer on the earth (Genesis 4:12). Yet God also placed a mark on Cain so that no one who found him would kill him (Genesis 4:15). Even in judgment, God protected him.

The story of Cain and Abel shows that free will is both a gift and a responsibility. Cain had the freedom to bring his best to God and to master his anger, but he chose otherwise. The warning God gave Cain still speaks to us: sin crouches at the door of every human heart, but we must decide whether to let it in or to overcome it. Free will makes us accountable for our choices, and it reminds us that obedience begins in the heart.

The Spread of Sin

The story of Cain and Abel was not an isolated event. As generations passed, the Bible shows that human sin continued to spread. After Cain killed Abel, Adam and Eve had another son named Seth, and through him humanity continued to grow (Genesis 4:25). From Cain's line came cities, music, tools, and technology (Genesis 4:17–22).

These show the creativity and ability God had given people, but alongside progress came violence. One of Cain's descendants, Lamech, boasted to his wives that he had killed a man for wounding him and a young man for injuring him (Genesis 4:23–24). Instead of learning from Cain's mistake, Lamech glorified violence and revenge.

The Bible also records a genealogy in Genesis 5, showing how the earth became more populated. People lived long lives and had many children. With growth in number came growth in wickedness.

By the time we reach Genesis 6, we read one of the saddest statements in all of Scripture: "The Lord saw how great the wickedness of the human race had become on the earth, and that every inclination of the thoughts of the human heart was only evil all the time" (Genesis 6:5).

Free will, the gift that was meant to allow love and obedience, was being used instead for selfishness and violence.

Genesis 6 also contains a puzzling passage about "the sons of God" and "the daughters of humans" (Genesis 6:1–2). While Bible readers interpret this in different ways, the point is clear: the boundaries God had set were being ignored. Humanity was living without regard for

His design, following desire instead of His will. The result was a world so corrupt that God declared, "I regret that I have made them" (Genesis 6:7).

Yet even in this dark moment, one man chose differently. Genesis 6:9 describes Noah as "a righteous man, blameless among the people of his time, and he walked faithfully with God." This shows again the power of free will. While the majority chose wickedness, Noah chose obedience. His decision would become the turning point in the story, for God would preserve humanity through him.

The spread of sin reveals how quickly human choices can shape society. From one lie in the garden came murder, then vengeance, then a world filled with violence. Free will is not only personal but also communal — the decisions of one generation affect the next. Yet the story also reminds us that even in the darkest times, God looks for those who will choose His way, just as Noah did.

The Great Flood

We have talked about the Great Flood in the previous two chapters. But it is an essential Biblical teaching that needs to be emphasized.

By the time of Noah, the world had become filled with violence and corruption. Genesis tells us, "Now the earth was corrupt in God's sight and was full of violence" (Genesis 6:11). People used their freedom not to honor God but to harm one another. Instead of choosing life, they chose selfishness, greed, and cruelty.

God looked on the earth and saw that humanity had twisted the gift of free will into something destructive.

God's response was both grief and judgment. "The Lord regretted that he had made human beings on the earth, and his heart was deeply troubled" (Genesis 6:6). This does not mean God had made a mistake; rather, it shows the depth of His sorrow. Sin was not only breaking rules; it was breaking His heart. Because of this, God announced that He would bring a flood to wipe away the corruption (Genesis 6:7).

But the story does not end with destruction. Genesis 6:8 says, "But Noah found favor in the eyes of the Lord." Unlike the rest of his generation, Noah chose to walk with God. When God told him to build an ark, Noah obeyed without question, even though the task was enormous and the warning must have seemed strange (Genesis 6:22). For years, he built the ark, a giant boat large enough to hold his family and pairs of every kind of animal.

His obedience was an act of faith and free will, in sharp contrast to the disobedience of the world around him.

When the floodwaters came, they covered the earth for forty days and forty nights (Genesis 7:12). Everything that had breath of life outside the ark perished (Genesis 7:21–23). It was a sobering reminder that choices have consequences. Humanity had chosen violence, and God allowed judgment to fall. Yet Noah and his family were spared because of their faith and obedience.

After the waters receded, Noah built an altar to the Lord and offered sacrifices (Genesis 8:20). God accepted Noah's worship and made a covenant, promising never again to destroy the earth with a flood. As a sign of this covenant, He placed a rainbow in the sky: "Whenever the rainbow appears in the clouds, I will see it and remember the everlasting covenant between God and all living creatures" (Genesis 9:16). The rainbow became a reminder of both God's justice and His mercy.

The flood story makes one thing clear: free will is powerful. Entire societies can choose violence and reap destruction, but one person's choice to follow God can preserve life and change history.

Noah's obedience saved not only his family but the future of humanity. His example calls each of us to consider how we will use the freedom God has given us. Will we follow the path of corruption, or will we, like Noah, choose to walk faithfully with God?

Unfortunately, the story of Noah does not end with the rainbow. Genesis 9:20–21 tells us that Noah planted a vineyard, drank some of the wine, and became drunk, lying uncovered in his tent. His son

Ham saw him and told his brothers, while Shem and Japheth walked in backward and covered their father respectfully (Genesis 9:22–23). When Noah awoke, he cursed Canaan, Ham's son, and blessed Shem and Japheth (Genesis 9:24–27).

This event reminds us that sin did not disappear after the Flood. Even a righteous man like Noah stumbled, and his sons faced choices of respect or dishonor. Free will was still at work, and once again humanity showed both failure and faithfulness. The message is clear: judgment through the Flood could not cleanse the human heart. Only God's grace could do that.

Chapter 4

COVENANT AND COMMANDMENTS:

GOD'S LAW FOR HIS PEOPLE

As you know by now, the Bible teaches that God's laws do not change (Malachi 3:6, Hebrews 13:8). From the beginning of creation until today, God's commandments, decrees, and statutes have remained constant. What changes is not God's Word but humanity's response to it. People again and again have used their free will to walk away from what God has commanded.

We saw this in the previous chapter, in the garden, when Adam and Eve were told not to eat from the tree of the knowledge of good and evil (Genesis 2:17). The command was clear, but they chose disobedience. We saw it in Cain, who was warned to master his anger (Genesis 4:7), but chose to kill his brother instead. We saw it in the generations before the Flood, where "every inclination of the thoughts of the human heart was only evil all the time" (Genesis 6:5). In each case, God's command did not change. What changed was how people responded.

This is one of the great lessons for understanding the Bible. It is not simply a collection of stories; it is the record of God's unchanging Word and humanity's varied responses to it. Each narrative shows us the tension between divine law and human freedom. God provides clear instruction, but He also provides choice. His commands are life-giving, but He does not force anyone to obey. Instead, He sets before people the opportunity to love Him freely.

As we move deeper into the story of Scripture, we will see how God chose a people to live under His covenant. He called Abraham to leave his home and trust Him. He gave the descendants of Abraham His law through Moses. These moments reveal not only God's plan for salvation but also the seriousness of free will. To follow God's laws is to walk in life; to reject them is to walk in disobedience.

The Bible is clear on this choice. Deuteronomy 30:19 says, "I have set before you life and death, blessings and curses. Now choose life, so that you and your children may live." The words given to Israel thousands of years ago still speak to us today. Free will means that every generation must decide whether to trust God's unchanging Word or to ignore it. The decision is never forced but always laid before us.

God Calls Abraham

After the great flood, humans once again grew and spread across the earth. They built cities, established kingdoms, and developed cultures. Yet, as before, many chose to live without regard for God's ways. Into this world God spoke to a man named Abram, later called Abraham. His story begins in Genesis 12, which is one of the most important turning points in the Bible.

God said to Abram, "Go from your country, your people, and your father's household to the land I will show you. I will make you into a great nation, and I will bless you; I will make your name great, and you will be a blessing" (Genesis 12:1–2).

Rather than starting over with all of humanity at once, God chose one man and his family as the foundation of a people who would know Him and carry His blessing to the world.

Here again, we see the theme of free will. God gave him a choice. He could stay in the security of his homeland, surrounded by his people and customs, or he could step out into the unknown, trusting God's promise.

Abram chose to obey: "So Abram went, as the Lord had told him" (Genesis 12:4). This act of obedience is why Abraham is often called the "father of faith." He did not know where he was going, but he trusted the One who called him.

Understanding this story helps us see how the Bible teaches about God's law and human response. There were no written commandments yet. Abraham only had God's voice and His promise.

His obedience was not about following a list of rules but about trusting God's word with his life. This sets a pattern for all who would follow: God speaks, humanity chooses, and free will makes faith real. Without the freedom to say no, Abraham's yes would not have been meaningful.

Abraham's decision also teaches us about God's larger plan. Through one man's faith, God promised to bring blessing to "all peoples on earth" (Genesis 12:3). This points forward to the way God's plan would ultimately include not only Israel but every nation. The call of Abraham shows that God's unchanging law is always tied to His purpose of love and redemption.

For readers of the Bible, Abraham's story is a reminder that God still calls people today. His voice may not command us to leave our homeland, but His Word calls us to trust Him, to walk in obedience, and to be a blessing to others.

Every act of faith, whether small or great, begins with the same choice Abraham faced: will we trust God's promise, or will we stay with what feels safe? Free will makes the answer to that question significant for every generation.

God makes a Covenant

Abraham's journey of faith did not end with leaving his homeland. God continued to speak to him and gradually revealed a covenant that would shape not only Abraham's life but the entire story of the Bible.

A covenant is more than a promise; it is a binding agreement between God and His people. It reveals God's law, His expectations, and His blessings for those who obey.

The Covenant Confirmed (Genesis 15)

In Genesis 15, Abraham worried that he had no heir. He asked God, "Sovereign Lord, what can you give me since I remain childless…?" (Genesis 15:2). God responded by taking him outside and saying, "Look up at the sky and count the stars—if indeed you can count them. So shall your offspring be" (Genesis 15:5). Abraham believed God, and the Bible says, "He credited it to him as righteousness" (Genesis 15:6). This is one of the clearest examples of how faith is counted as obedience. Abraham did not earn God's favor by works; he trusted God's word, and that trust was pleasing to God.

This moment also connects to free will. Abraham could have chosen to doubt. He was old, and his wife, Sarah, was beyond childbearing age. From a human perspective, the promise seemed impossible. But Abraham used his freedom to believe. His faith teaches us that obedience begins with trust in God's word, even when circumstances look hopeless.

The Sign of the Covenant (Genesis 17)

Years later, God expanded on His covenant with Abraham in Genesis 17. He changed his name from Abram ("exalted father") to Abraham ("father of many nations") and gave circumcision as the sign of the covenant. God said, "This is my covenant with you and your descendants after you… Every male among you shall be circumcised" (Genesis 17:10). This physical sign marked Abraham's family as God's chosen people.

For readers today, circumcision may seem like a strange or unnecessary requirement. But in the Bible, it symbolized obedience and belonging. It was an outward sign of an inward commitment. The principle remains important: God calls His people to live in visible ways that reflect their faith. Free will means they could choose to accept the covenant sign or reject it. To obey was to live under God's law and blessing; to disobey was to step outside of it.

The Test of Isaac (Genesis 22)

Perhaps the greatest test of Abraham's faith came in Genesis 22. God told him, "Take your son, your only son, whom you love—Isaac—and go to the region of Moriah. Sacrifice him there as a burnt offering" (Genesis 22:2). This command must have shaken Abraham to his core. Isaac was the child of promise, the one through whom God had said his descendants would come. Yet Abraham obeyed. He took Isaac to the mountain, built an altar, and prepared to offer him.

At the last moment, God stopped him: "Do not lay a hand on the boy... Now I know that you fear God, because you have not withheld from me your son, your only son" (Genesis 22:12). Instead of Isaac, God provided a ram caught in the thicket, and Abraham offered it in his place (Genesis 22:13). This event revealed Abraham's complete trust and foreshadowed the ultimate sacrifice of Christ, the Lamb of God who would die in our place.

The story of Isaac again underscores free will. Abraham could have refused. He could have argued with God or turned away. Instead, he obeyed, and his obedience became a testimony for generations. James 2:22 explains, "His faith and his actions were working together, and his faith was made complete by what he did." Faith is not only what we believe but also how we act on God's word.

Understanding the Bible with the Covenant

Abraham's covenant shows us how God's unchanging laws meet human freedom. God established promises, signs, and commands, but Abraham had to choose whether to accept them. His faith did not make him perfect—he stumbled more than once—but his overall pattern was obedience. Through Abraham, we learn that God's law is not given to crush us but to invite us into a relationship.

This covenant also helps us understand the Bible as a whole. The promises to Abraham run like a golden thread through the entire story of Scripture. The land, the people, and the blessing find their fulfillment in Jesus Christ, who came as Abraham's descendant and the Savior of all nations. Galatians 3:29 declares, "If you belong to Christ, then you are Abraham's seed, and heirs according to the promise."

Israel and the Law

The story of Abraham's descendants continues with the birth of the nation of Israel. After centuries of slavery in Egypt, God raised up Moses to deliver His people.

Through a series of mighty signs, including the parting of the Red Sea, He brought them out of bondage and led them toward the land He had promised to Abraham. Yet freedom from Egypt was only the beginning. God had not simply rescued them from slavery; He had rescued them for a purpose: to live as His people under His law.

In Exodus 19, the Israelites camped at the base of Mount Sinai. There God descended in fire and cloud, and the mountain shook with His presence. Out of this awesome display, God spoke the Ten Commandments (Exodus 20:1–17).

These commandments became the foundation of Israel's covenant life. They began with God's relationship to His people: "I am the Lord your God, who brought you out of Egypt, out of the land of slavery" (Exodus 20:2). Then followed commands to worship Him alone, to keep His name holy, and to honor the Sabbath. The commandments also addressed how people should treat one another: honoring parents, rejecting murder, adultery, theft, false testimony, and coveting.

The Ten Commandments reveal God's unchanging standards. They show His holiness and His desire for His people to reflect that holiness in their lives. These laws were not given as suggestions but as binding instructions. Yet they also reflected God's mercy: He gave His people clear direction so they would know how to live in a way that brought life rather than destruction.

The Law and Free Will

Even with these clear commandments, God did not take away the people's freedom. They were called to choose whether they would obey.

Deuteronomy 30:19 captures this choice in powerful words: "This day I call the heavens and the earth as witnesses against you that I have set before you life and death, blessings and curses.

Now choose life, so that you and your children may live." Free will remained at the heart of the covenant. God laid out the blessings of obedience and the consequences of disobedience, but He left the decision in the people's hands.

This truth is essential for understanding the Bible. God never forces Himself on humanity. He reveals His will and calls for obedience, but He allows His people to make their own choices.

In doing so, He shows respect for the freedom He gave them at creation. Just as Adam and Eve had to decide whether to obey God in the garden, and just as Abraham had to decide whether to trust God's promises, so the people of Israel had to decide whether to follow God's law.

God also commanded Israel to pass His laws down faithfully. In Deuteronomy 6:6-7, Moses told the people, "These commandments that I give you today are to be on your hearts. Impress them on your children. Talk about them when you sit at home and when you walk along the road, when you lie down and when you get up."

Obedience was not only an individual choice but a community responsibility. Parents were called to teach their children, and the whole nation was called to live in such a way that the surrounding peoples would see the wisdom of God's laws.

This reminds us that free will is not exercised in isolation. Our choices affect families, communities, and even future generations. Israel's obedience or disobedience would shape the destiny of their children and determine their witness to the nations around them.

The Law as a Mirror

Finally, the law served as a mirror. It showed Israel who God is and who they were meant to be. But it also revealed how far short they fell. Romans 3:20 explains, "Through the law we become conscious of our sin."

The commandments made it clear what obedience looked like, but they also made disobedience undeniable. This tension runs throughout the Old Testament: the law is perfect, but the people are not. Free will gives them the choice to obey, but too often they choose rebellion.

The law was never meant to be a burden but a gift. When God gave Israel His commandments, He was showing them how to live in a way that reflected His character and brought life. Psalm 19:7 says, "The law of the Lord is perfect, refreshing the soul." God's law revealed His holiness, but it also provided a pathway for His people to experience blessing.

The first purpose of the law was to reveal God's will. Without the law, people could only guess at what God required. The commandments made it plain: love God above all, and love your neighbor as yourself (summarized later by Jesus in Matthew 22:37-40). In this way, the law was a light to guide God's people in every part of life.

The second purpose was to show the seriousness of sin. Romans 7:7 explains, "I would not have known what sin was had it not been for the law." The commandments made clear that disobedience was not just a mistake but rebellion against God.

Every time Israel failed to live up to God's law, they were reminded that free will carries responsibility. Choices have consequences, both for the individual and for the community.

The third purpose was to point to the need for God's mercy.

Israel's repeated failures under the law revealed that no one could keep it perfectly. This was not a flaw in the law but a reflection of the human heart.

Galatians 3:24 says, "The law was our guardian until Christ came that we might be justified by faith." The law was never the final answer. It prepared the way for the Savior who would fulfill it perfectly.

For those learning to understand the Bible, this truth is essential: the law shows us what God requires, reveals our need for forgiveness, and points us to the grace of God in Christ. It was a gift to Israel and remains a teacher for us today.

But Israel's history of disobedience is a long one, requiring a chapter of its own.

Chapter 5

COVENANT, KINGDOM, AND DISOBEDIENCE

When God brought the Israelites out of Egypt, He freed them from slavery and gave them a new identity. He wanted them to become a nation with a special purpose.

At Mount Sinai, God told Moses, "Now if you obey me fully and keep my covenant, then out of all nations you will be my treasured possession… you will be for me a kingdom of priests and a holy nation" (Exodus 19:5–6). This means that Israel's role was to be different from the nations around them. And God wanted their way of life to display His wisdom and holiness.

This was a unique calling. Other nations looked to kings, armies, or idols to guide them. Israel had God Himself as their ruler. He gave them commandments and laws so they would know exactly what pleased Him. The Ten Commandments stood at the center of these laws. They taught the people how to love God and how to treat one another with respect.

Even though God gave clear instructions, He also gave His people freedom to obey them. From the beginning of creation, God allowed humans to make choices.

He gave Adam and Eve the ability to choose. He gave Abraham the ability to choose. In the same way, Israel had the freedom to follow or to turn away. Obedience would bring blessing. Disobedience would bring consequences. These choices shaped the future of the entire nation.

Moses explained this before they entered the Promised Land: "See, I set before you today life and prosperity, death and destruction" (Deuteronomy 30:15). God wanted His people to see that His laws gave them life. If they rejected Him, they would face ruin.

This is the main theme of Israel's history. It was not only about battles, kings, or prophets. It was about people struggling between God's perfect law and their own disobedience. Again and again, they chose their own way. Again and again, God called them back. Their story is also our story. We have been given free will. We have God's Word to guide us. And we face the same choice: to obey Him or to walk away.

Israel's story as God's chosen nation began with deliverance from Egypt. But once they entered the wilderness, a deeper struggle began.

Their journey to the Promised Land could have been short, yet it stretched to forty years because they repeatedly disobeyed. The wilderness became the place where God's law met human free will.

The Golden Calf

One of the earliest failures happened at Mount Sinai. Moses went up the mountain to meet with God and receive His commandments. While Moses was gone, the people grew restless. They gathered around Aaron, Moses' brother, and demanded, "Come, make us gods who will go before us" (Exodus 32:1). Aaron made a golden calf, and the people worshiped it with feasting and celebration.

This was a direct violation of God's commandments. He had already told them, "You shall have no other gods before me. You shall not make for yourself an image" (Exodus 20:3–4). Instead of waiting for God's word through Moses, they took matters into their own hands. They chose something they could see and touch rather than trusting the God who had rescued them from slavery. The golden calf showed how quickly people can trade devotion for disobedience when they follow their own desires.

Grumbling in the Desert

The wilderness was also filled with constant complaints. In Numbers 11, the people grumbled about their hardships and longed for the food they had eaten in Egypt. God had given them manna from heaven each morning (Exodus 16:4). Still, they grew tired of it and said, "We never see anything but this manna!" (Numbers 11:6). Instead of being grateful for God's daily provision, they chose to focus on what they did not have.

Later, when they came to the border of the Promised Land, twelve men were sent to scout the territory (Numbers 13). Ten of them returned with fearful reports about giants and fortified cities. Only Joshua and Caleb encouraged the people to trust God's promise and move forward. The nation refused. They cried out, rebelled against Moses, and even talked about going back to Egypt (Numbers 14:1–4). Because they rejected God's word, they were sentenced to wander in the desert for forty years.

Free Will and Consequences

These stories highlight the power of human choice. God had rescued Israel with miracles, parted the Red Sea, and provided food and water in the desert. He gave them His laws and stayed close to them with a pillar of cloud by day and fire by night (Exodus 13:21–22). Yet the people still turned away again and again. Their freedom to choose remained, even as God's people, and that freedom became the stage on which their covenant relationship was tested.

For us today, these wilderness stories carry an important lesson. Following God is not only about seeing miracles or hearing clear instructions. It is about daily decisions to trust Him and to give thanks. Israel had everything they needed to remain faithful, yet they mostly chose another path.

Their story reminds us that free will is a gift. But like all gifts, it must be used with care and wisdom.

The Promised Land and the Judges

After forty years in the wilderness, the Israelites finally stepped into the land God had promised to their ancestors. Under Joshua's leadership, they crossed the Jordan River and began to claim Canaan as their home. At this moment of fulfillment, God reminded them of His covenant.

Their future in the land would depend on obedience. Blessing would follow faithfulness, but destruction would come through disobedience. Joshua made the challenge personal when he declared, "Choose for yourselves this day whom you will serve... But as for me and my household, we will serve the Lord" (Joshua 24:15).

Receiving the land was not the conclusion of Israel's journey. It was the beginning of a new chapter filled with responsibility. The land was fertile, abundant, and everything their ancestors had longed for (Deuteronomy 6:10-11).

Yet the real test was not farming the soil or building homes. It was whether they would remain faithful to God in the midst of plenty. Even surrounded by blessings, the people still had to decide each day whom they would serve.

For a time, under Joshua's leadership, the nation stayed faithful (Joshua 24:31). But once he died, everything began to change. A new generation rose up that "knew neither the Lord nor what he had done for Israel" (Judges 2:10). Without living memory of God's deliverance, their loyalty quickly faded. What followed was a painful cycle that defined the entire period of the judges.

The book of Judges describes this cycle in clear terms. First, the Israelites abandoned God's commands and worshiped idols.

As a consequence, God allowed foreign nations to oppress them. In their suffering, the people cried out for mercy. God answered by raising up judges — leaders who delivered them and restored peace.

But once stability returned, the people drifted back into disobedience, and the cycle began again.

This repeated pattern shows how fragile their faithfulness was. Judges 21:25 summarizes the situation with blunt honesty: "In those days Israel had no king; everyone did as they saw fit." Their free will was real, but without devotion to God, it produced disorder instead of freedom.

The time of the judges makes one truth clear: changing outward circumstances does not change the human heart.

Even the judges themselves reflected this tension. Deborah (Judges 4–5) and Gideon (Judges 6–8) trusted God and led with courage. Samson (Judges 13–16) was strong but often driven by selfish desires. Whether the leaders were faithful or flawed, the people's own choices ultimately determined the outcome. Again and again, free will became the dividing line between obedience and rebellion.

Kings and Kingdoms

After the time of the judges, Israel wanted stability. They looked at the nations around them and noticed that every nation had a king to lead them. The elders of Israel came to the prophet Samuel and demanded the same: "Appoint a king to lead us, such as all the other nations have" (1 Samuel 8:5). This was not just a request for leadership. It was a rejection of God's direct rule over His people. God told Samuel, "They have rejected me as their king" (1 Samuel 8:7).

Saul: A King of the People's Choice

God gave Israel what they asked for by appointing Saul as their first king. Saul looked like the kind of leader people wanted. He was tall, strong, and outwardly impressive (1 Samuel 9:2). At first, Saul showed courage in battle and seemed like the right choice.

But soon he disobeyed God. In one situation, Saul grew impatient waiting for Samuel and performed a sacrifice that only a priest or prophet was allowed to make (1 Samuel 13). Later, God told him to destroy the Amalekites, one of Israel's enemies, completely, but Saul kept some of their animals and spared their king (1 Samuel 15).

Because of this repeated disobedience, God rejected Saul as king. Saul's story shows how choosing to ignore God's instructions can ruin even the strongest beginning.

David: A Man After God's Heart

After Saul, God chose David to be king. David was the youngest son in his family and worked as a shepherd in Bethlehem. Unlike Saul, he was not chosen for his size or appearance. God told Samuel, "The Lord does not look at the things people look at. People look at the outward appearance, but the Lord looks at the heart" (1 Samuel 16:7).

David's trust in God became clear in one of the most famous events in the Bible. When Israel faced the Philistines, their enemy army, a giant named Goliath challenged them to single combat. Goliath was over nine feet tall and terrified everyone. David, armed only with a sling and a few stones, trusted God to give him victory. With one stone, he struck Goliath on the forehead and killed him (1 Samuel 17). This moment showed David's faith and courage.

Later, as king, David wrote psalms — songs and prayers that worshiped God — and often sought God's guidance.

Yet David also misused his freedom. He saw Bathsheba, the wife of a soldier named Uriah, and committed adultery with her (2 Samuel 11). To cover it up, he arranged for Uriah to be killed in battle.

This was one of David's greatest failures. But when the prophet Nathan confronted him, David admitted his sin and asked for God's mercy, writing words like those found in Psalm 51: "Create in me a pure heart, O God, and renew a steadfast spirit within me." David's life shows that obedience is not about perfection. It is about turning back to God with a repentant heart when we fall.

Solomon: Wisdom and Failure

David's son Solomon became the next king. When God asked Solomon what he wanted most, Solomon asked for wisdom. God answered, "I will give you a wise and discerning heart" (1 Kings 3:12). Solomon's wisdom became famous, and leaders from other nations came to hear his judgments. During his reign, Israel became wealthy and powerful. Solomon also built the temple in Jerusalem, a magnificent place of worship where the people gathered to honor God (1 Kings 8).

But Solomon's devotion did not last. He married many foreign wives, and they brought their idols into Israel. Over time, Solomon began worshiping those false gods alongside the Lord (1 Kings 11:4). His story reminds us that wisdom alone is not enough. Free will is a daily test, and even the wisest person can fall if their heart turns away from God.

After Solomon's death, the kingdom was split into two. The northern tribes formed the kingdom of Israel, and the southern tribes formed the kingdom of Judah (1 Kings 12). Both kingdoms struggled with idolatry — the worship of other gods — and with injustice. Most of their kings led the people into sin. A few, like Hezekiah and Josiah, tried to restore faithfulness to God (2 Kings 18:3; 22:2). But overall, the story of the divided kingdom shows how the disobedience of leaders spreads to the people they rule. The choices of kings shaped the future of entire generations.

The history of the kings teaches that no human leader can take the place of God. Israel wanted to be like other nations, but what they truly needed was faithfulness to the Lord.

Even the best kings stumbled, and the worst kings led the nation into disaster. The message is consistent: God's commands stay the same, but human hearts often wander. The kings remind us that free will is powerful — it can lead to blessing when used in obedience, or to ruin when turned toward disobedience.

Prophets and Warnings

As Israel's kings led the people deeper into disobedience, God did not remain silent. Out of His mercy, He raised up prophets to speak His word, call the nation to repentance, and warn of coming judgment. Prophets were not fortune-tellers but messengers of God. They reminded the people of the covenant and pleaded with them to turn back before it was too late.

One of the most famous prophets was Elijah. During the reign of King Ahab, who promoted the worship of Baal, Elijah stood alone on Mount Carmel and challenged the people: "How long will you waver between two opinions? If the Lord is God, follow him; but if Baal is God, follow him" (1 Kings 18:21). The people's free will was once again at the center. God had shown His power, but they had to choose whether they would serve Him or idols.

Isaiah also spoke to Judah, warning them of their sin but also offering hope. He declared God's grief over their rebellion: "Woe to the sinful nation, a people whose guilt is great, a brood of evildoers" (Isaiah 1:4). Yet Isaiah also pointed forward to God's plan of salvation through the coming Messiah: "The people walking in darkness have seen a great light" (Isaiah 9:2). Through Isaiah, we see how the prophets both confronted sin and prepared the way for Christ.

Jeremiah, sometimes called the "weeping prophet," lived during the final days before Judah's exile to Babylon. He urged the people to return to God: "Obey me, and I will be your God and you will be my people" (Jeremiah 7:23). But the people refused. Instead, they hardened their hearts and rejected the prophets. Their free will was used to resist God's call, and the result was national destruction.

Despite their warnings, most prophets were ignored or persecuted. Yet their message reveals an important truth about God's unchanging law. Even when His people disobey, He continues to speak. He does not abandon them without warning. He pleads, He instructs, and He calls them back. But He will not force obedience. Free will remains at the heart of the covenant relationship.

For readers today, the prophets teach us how to understand the Bible's bigger story. Israel's history shows that laws, kings, and prophets could not permanently change the human heart. Again and again, people chose disobedience.

Yet woven through the warnings is a message of hope. God promised a new covenant, written not on tablets of stone but on human hearts (Jeremiah 31:33). This promise pointed forward to Christ, who would fulfill the law and provide the power to obey truly.

Israel's Lesson for Us

The story of Israel — from wilderness to judges, from kings to prophets — is the story of a nation wrestling with free will under God's law. Sometimes they chose obedience, and blessing followed. More often, they chose disobedience, and judgment came. Yet in every stage, God remained faithful. He gave them His word, sent them leaders, and raised up prophets to warn and guide them.

Understanding the Bible means seeing Israel's history not just as the rise and fall of a nation but as a mirror for humanity. Their choices are our choices. Their struggles reveal the same tension we face today: will we obey God's unchanging word, or will we turn aside to our own ways? The prophets show us that while disobedience brings consequences, God never stops calling His people back.

Chapter 6

EXILE AND RETURN: HOPE OF A NEW COVENANT

The story of Israel's kings and prophets ended with a sobering reality. Despite God's patience and the repeated warnings of His messengers, the people continued to misuse their free will. Kings led them into idolatry, but prophets called them back; yet, the nation as a whole continued to choose disobedience.

Their failure grew into a recurring pattern across generations. By the end of Israel's kingdom era (around 586 BC), the covenant relationship that had once been marked by blessing was overshadowed by judgment.

God had made the terms clear from the beginning: "If you obey me fully and keep my covenant, then out of all nations you will be my treasured possession" (Exodus 19:5).

He had also warned of the consequences of disobedience: "If you do not obey the Lord your God... you will be uprooted from the land you are entering to possess" (Deuteronomy 28:15, 63). Israel had been given God's law, His prophets, and His presence, yet free will meant they could still turn away from Him. And that is precisely what happened.

The result was the exile. In 2 Kings 25, we see the culmination of centuries of rebellion. The Babylonian armies surrounded Jerusalem, broke through its walls, and set fire to the temple, the very place where God's name had dwelled.

The people were carried away into captivity, their homes destroyed, their land lost. The book of Lamentations gives voice to this grief:

"How deserted lies the city, once so full of people! How like a widow is she, who once was great among the nations!" (Lamentations 1:1).

The exile came as the natural consequence of free will misused on a national scale. Israel's persistent disobedience brought them to the point where God allowed them to face the results of their choices.

This is one of the most important lessons for understanding the Bible: God's laws remain constant, and His covenant promises of blessing and warning are equally valid. Free will gives humanity the dignity of choice, but every choice carries responsibility.

Even in the darkest hour, God's faithfulness continued. His people were scattered and His temple destroyed, yet His word endured.

The exile marked a turning point in their story. It stood as a painful reminder that obedience leads to life, disobedience leads to death, and human effort alone cannot provide hope. In this season of despair, the promise of a new covenant began to shine more clearly, preparing the way for Christ.

Life in Exile

Exile was the shattering of Israel's identity. The temple was gone, the city walls broken down, and the people scattered across Babylon and other foreign lands.

For a nation called to be "a kingdom of priests and a holy nation" (Exodus 19:6), the loss of land, temple, and king was devastating. They had to face the question: How do we remain God's people when everything familiar is gone?

The prophets had warned that exile would be the consequence of disobedience. Yet within that judgment, the exile also became a new test of free will. Would the people cling to God even in a foreign land, or would they give in to the pressures of assimilation?

This tension is captured in Psalm 137:1-2, where the exiles lament, "By the rivers of Babylon we sat and wept when we remembered

Zion. There on the poplars we hung our harps." Grief was real, but faithfulness was an even greater challenge.

Daniel and His Friends

The book of Daniel gives us a window into what faithful obedience looked like in exile. Daniel and his friends were taken into the Babylonian court, trained in its language and literature (Daniel 1:4). Yet when they were offered royal food and wine, they resolved not to defile themselves (Daniel 1:8). They chose obedience to God's dietary laws over compromise, even though it carried risk. Their free will was tested, and they chose faithfulness.

Later, Daniel's friends Shadrach, Meshach, and Abednego faced the command to bow down to a golden image. They refused, declaring, "The God we serve can deliver us… But even if he does not, we want you to know… we will not serve your gods" (Daniel 3:17–18). Their choice led them into the fiery furnace, yet God delivered them unharmed. Their story shows that obedience may bring suffering, but it always demonstrates trust in God.

Daniel himself faced a similar test when a royal decree forbade prayer to anyone except the king. Still, Daniel prayed three times a day to the Lord, as he had always done (Daniel 6:10). For his faithfulness, he was thrown into the lions' den, but God shut the lions' mouths and preserved his life. Again, free will was the deciding factor: Daniel could have hidden his devotion, yet he chose open obedience to God's law.

These stories highlight the role of free will in exile. Even far from their land and temple, God's people still had the choice to obey or disobey. The external circumstances had changed, but the core question remained the same: would they live according to God's law or the ways of the world around them? The examples of Daniel and his friends show that obedience is possible even under pressure, and that God honors those who remain faithful.

The exile teaches us that God's presence is not confined to a place. Even when the temple lay in ruins, He was still with His people.

Faithfulness no longer depended on sacrifices in Jerusalem; it was expressed through obedience in daily life.

This helps us understand the Bible's larger story: God desires hearts that choose Him freely, whether in a land of blessing or in a land of captivity. The exile reminds us that God's people are defined not by geography or buildings but by obedience to His unchanging word.

Prophetic Hope During Exile

Though the exile was a time of profound loss, it was not without hope. Even as Jerusalem lay in ruins and the people were scattered, God continued to speak through His prophets. The message of exile was not only judgment but also restoration. God used the darkest season of Israel's history to reveal His plan for a new covenant and a greater redemption to come.

Jeremiah: A New Covenant

Before the exile began, Jeremiah warned the people of God's judgment. But in the midst of those warnings, he also spoke of hope. In Jeremiah 31:31–33, God said, "The days are coming when I will make a new covenant with the people of Israel and with the people of Judah… I will put my law in their minds and write it on their hearts. I will be their God, and they will be my people."

This promise showed that the problem was not with God's law but with the human heart. Israel had misused their free will again and again, proving that no amount of external commands could guarantee obedience. What they needed was an inward transformation. Jeremiah's vision pointed forward to a covenant that would not depend on stone tablets or temple rituals but on God Himself changing the human heart.

Ezekiel: From Death to Life

Ezekiel, another prophet during the exile, received visions that emphasized God's power to restore. In Ezekiel 37:1–14, he saw a valley of dry bones that came to life when God's Spirit breathed into them.

This vision symbolized Israel, a nation "cut off" and without hope (Ezekiel 37:11). Yet God promised to bring them back to their land and give them His Spirit.

Ezekiel's vision is a vivid picture of what happens when God's people misuse their freedom. Disobedience leads to death, just as bones are lifeless. But God's Spirit can bring renewal and life where there was only despair. This helps us understand the Bible's message that hope is never lost, even when human choices have led to ruin.

Isaiah: The Suffering Servant

The prophet Isaiah, though he lived before the exile, spoke words that became especially meaningful during it. He prophesied about a Servant who would suffer for the sins of the people: "He was pierced for our transgressions, he was crushed for our iniquities… and by his wounds we are healed" (Isaiah 53:5).

This Servant, Christians later understood, pointed to Jesus Christ, who would bear the punishment of disobedience and bring forgiveness.

Isaiah's message gave hope that God's plan was bigger than Israel's failure. Free will had led the nation into exile, but God's love would not abandon them there. His Servant would one day take the consequences of sin on Himself, opening the way for genuine reconciliation.

Together, the voices of Jeremiah, Ezekiel, and Isaiah remind us that God's judgment is never the final word. Exile was painful, but it prepared God's people for something greater.

It taught them that obedience requires more than rituals or leaders; it requires a transformed heart. It pointed them forward to the coming of Christ, who would fulfill the law and bring the Spirit to live within His people.

Return and Rebuilding

After seventy years in Babylon, God stirred the heart of a foreign king to begin Israel's return. The book of Ezra opens with these words:

"In the first year of Cyrus king of Persia… the Lord moved the heart of Cyrus… to make a proclamation throughout his realm and also to put it in writing: 'The Lord, the God of heaven, has given me all the kingdoms of the earth and he has appointed me to build a temple for him at Jerusalem'" (Ezra 1:1–2). What the prophets had foretold came to pass. God brought His people back, just as He had promised.

Rebuilding the Temple

Under the leadership of Zerubbabel, the people laid the foundation of a new temple (Ezra 3:10–11). For those who remembered Solomon's temple, the new building seemed small by comparison. Still, the prophet Haggai encouraged them that the glory of this house would surpass the former (Haggai 2:9). The temple represented God's presence with His people. Its rebuilding was a powerful sign of restoration.

Even so, obedience was fragile. Opposition from surrounding peoples discouraged the work, and for a time, construction stopped (Ezra 4:4–5). The people needed constant reminders from prophets like Haggai and Zechariah to persevere. Free will still shaped the outcome: God had opened the way for return, yet the people had to choose whether to walk in faith.

Later, Nehemiah, a Jewish official serving in Persia, heard that Jerusalem's walls were still broken down. Grieved, he sought permission from King Artaxerxes to rebuild them. Nehemiah faced opposition and threats, but he led the people with courage and determination. In just fifty-two days, the walls were rebuilt (Nehemiah 6:15). This remarkable achievement showed what perseverance and obedience could accomplish when aligned with God's will.

The return also brought disappointment. Even after the temple and walls were restored, the people continued to falter. Nehemiah records how they neglected the Sabbath, intermarried with foreign nations, and failed to support the temple properly (Nehemiah 13). Their hearts strayed despite all that God had done for them.

Exile had not cured the deeper problem. Free will still remained, along with the temptation to disobey. Structures could rise again, but the human heart still required transformation.

The return from exile reminds us that outward restoration cannot reach the root of the issue. God's people had their land, their temple, and their city walls again, but they still needed something greater — a covenant written on their hearts.

These points forward to the Bible's movement toward Christ. The Old Testament closes with a restored people still longing for complete renewal. Their story shows that human effort can rebuild walls, yet only God can rebuild hearts.

Lessons of the Exile

The exile stands as one of the most crucial turning points in the Bible. It showed the people of Israel, and us as readers today, that God's law is unchanging and His covenant warnings are accurate. For generations, the prophets had warned of judgment, and at last the warnings came to pass. But the exile also revealed several key lessons that help us understand the Bible.

First, it shows the seriousness of free will. God did not force Israel into obedience. He gave them the dignity of choice, and they misused it. Their disobedience led to ruin, but their repentance in exile also showed that free will can turn hearts back toward God. The same freedom that leads to rebellion can also lead to restoration.

Second, it shows that outward religion cannot save. The people had the temple, the law, and their heritage, but none of these could guarantee obedience. What mattered was the condition of the heart. Exile exposed the truth that Israel needed more than priests, sacrifices, or kings — they needed transformation from within.

Third, the exile teaches us that God's love never fails, even in judgment. The destruction of Jerusalem was devastating, but even then

God spoke through Jeremiah, Ezekiel, and others, offering promises of restoration and hope. The exile was not the end of God's plan but a chapter in His greater purpose.

Chapter 7

THE FULFILLMENT OF THE PROMISE:

CHRIST THE NEW COVENANT

The return from exile gave Israel back its land, its city, and even its temple, but the deeper problem remained. Walls were rebuilt, yet hearts still wandered. Sacrifices resumed, yet the people continued to struggle to keep God's commandments. By the end of the Old Testament, the story feels unfinished. God's people were back in Jerusalem, yet the promises of the prophets pointed to something greater still.

Malachi, the last prophet of the Old Testament, spoke of a messenger who would prepare the way for the Lord Himself: "I will send my messenger, who will prepare the way before me. Then suddenly the Lord you are seeking will come to his temple" (Malachi 3:1). Centuries earlier, Isaiah had described a people "walking in darkness" who would see "a great light" (Isaiah 9:2). These words kept alive the hope that God's plan was still unfolding. A new covenant was still to come, one that would restore outward worship and transform the human heart.

This longing ran deep in Israel. Generations of failure under the law had shown that human effort could not succeed. Free will had again and again led to disobedience. The judges, kings, and prophets failed to solve the problem of sin. The exile proved that rejecting God's law carried consequences, and the return proved that the same pattern of rebellion persisted. The people needed more than laws or leaders; they needed a Savior.

For readers of the Bible, this is where the Old Testament leaves us: waiting. The story of creation, covenant, kingdom, exile, and return all point forward to a resolution yet to come. The stage was set for the arrival of Christ, the one who would fulfill the promises, embody God's law perfectly, and offer grace for the failures of human free will.

The Birth of Christ: God With Us

When the time came for God to fulfill His promises, He did so in an unexpected way. The Messiah arrived as a child, born in humble circumstances. Matthew's Gospel explains that this birth fulfilled Isaiah's prophecy: "The virgin will conceive and give birth to a son, and they will call him Immanuel," which means "God with us" (Matthew 1:22-23; Isaiah 7:14).

This truth is central to understanding the Bible. God was present, not sending laws or prophets from afar but entering the world Himself. The same God who gave His people commandments at Sinai came as a baby in Bethlehem. In Christ, God was with His people in the most personal way possible.

The birth of Christ also highlights the role of free will in God's plan. When the angel Gabriel told Mary that she would conceive by the Holy Spirit, she was troubled. Yet she answered, "I am the Lord's servant… May your word to me be fulfilled" (Luke 1:38). Mary chose obedience, even though it meant risk, misunderstanding, and hardship. Her willingness to trust God made her part of the fulfillment of His promises.

Joseph faced a similar choice. When he learned that Mary was pregnant, he planned to end their engagement quietly. But an angel appeared in a dream and told him, "Do not be afraid to take Mary home as your wife, because what is conceived in her is from the Holy Spirit" (Matthew 1:20). Joseph chose to obey, even when it defied human expectations.

These responses show how God works through human freedom. He does not override free will; instead, He invites people to trust Him. Mary and Joseph could have said no, but their yes became part of God's great plan of salvation.

The circumstances of Jesus' birth reveal God's heart. He was born in a stable. His first visitors were shepherds, people of low status, yet they were told, "Today in the town of David a Savior has been born to you; he is the Messiah, the Lord" (Luke 2:11). From the beginning, Christ's coming showed that God's salvation is for all people.

The birth of Christ is more than a historical event. It is the turning point of the Bible's story. The God whose laws had been ignored and whose prophets had been rejected chose to step into human history Himself. In Jesus, we see both the seriousness of sin and the greatness of God's love. Free will had led humanity astray, and in Christ, God made a way for obedience to be restored.

The Ministry of Jesus

After His birth and early years, the Gospels move quickly to the ministry of Jesus. At about thirty years old, He began preaching, teaching, and performing miracles that revealed the kingdom of God. His ministry focused on showing what it meant to live in obedience to God's will. In Him, the law and the prophets reached their fulfillment (Matthew 5:17).

From the beginning, Jesus declared His central message: "The time has come... The kingdom of God has come near. Repent and believe the good news!" (Mark 1:15).

This announcement set the tone for His ministry. The kingdom of God was the rule of God in the hearts of people who freely chose to follow Him. His call to "repent" meant turning away from disobedience and embracing obedience through faith.

One of Jesus' most famous teachings is the Sermon on the Mount (Matthew 5–7). In this sermon, He explained the deeper meaning of God's law. For example, the law said, "You shall not murder," and Jesus taught that even anger and insult bring guilt (Matthew 5:21-22). The law said, "Do not commit adultery," and Jesus explained that even lustful thoughts are sinful (Matthew 5:27-28).

By doing this, Jesus showed that obedience involves the heart as well as external actions. Free will goes beyond choosing what we do; it also shapes what we think and desire. Jesus called His followers to a higher standard of righteousness, one that no checklist of rules could capture and that reflected God's own holiness.

Jesus' miracles were signs of God's kingdom breaking into the world. He healed the sick, gave sight to the blind, fed the hungry, and even raised the dead. These acts expressed compassion. They showed that God's law of love was being lived out in action. When He healed a leper, He reached out and touched the man, saying, "Be clean!" (Mark 1:41). In doing so, He restored both body and dignity.

These miracles also confronted the misuse of free will. Some saw them and believed, while others saw the same signs and rejected Him. The miracles forced people to decide: would they acknowledge the kingdom of God, or would they turn away in disbelief?

Another central part of Jesus' ministry was calling disciples. He said to fishermen by the Sea of Galilee, "Come, follow me... and I will send you out to fish for people" (Matthew 4:19). They left their nets and followed Him.

This shows again how God respects human freedom. The call was clear, but the choice to follow was theirs. Some, like Peter and John, responded in obedience. Others, like the rich young ruler who refused to give up his wealth (Mark 10:21-22), chose disobedience.

Understanding the Bible Through Christ's Ministry

The ministry of Jesus helps us see the Bible's message more clearly. From creation to covenant to exile, humanity had misused its free will. Jesus came to show what perfect obedience looks like — a life lived entirely in harmony with God's will. His preaching, teaching, miracles, and call to discipleship all reveal that the kingdom of God is about transformed hearts and lives.

Christ and the Law

Throughout His ministry, Jesus was often confronted by the religious leaders of His day. The Pharisees and teachers of the law were experts in the commandments, yet Jesus showed that their approach had missed the heart of God's intention. His relationship with the law is one of the most important keys to understanding the Bible.

Jesus declared plainly, "Do not think that I have come to abolish the Law or the Prophets; I have not come to abolish them but to fulfill them" (Matthew 5:17).

This statement is important because it clarifies two common misunderstandings. Jesus was affirming the law given through Moses while also rejecting shallow obedience to rules. Instead, He brought the law to its true purpose: guiding people into a life that reflects God's holiness and love.

The Pharisees often focused on outward rituals such as fasting, tithing, and ceremonial washing, yet Jesus warned that such actions meant little if the heart was far from God. He quoted Isaiah, saying, "These people honor me with their lips, but their hearts are far from me" (Matthew 15:8). Obedience involves loving God with all one's heart, soul, and mind (Matthew 22:37).

This shows again the role of free will. Anyone can perform external acts without true devotion, but God desires willing obedience that flows from love. Jesus revealed that the law is a path to genuine life when embraced freely.

Jesus often exposed the hypocrisy of leaders who used the law to control others while excusing their own sin. He warned them, "You give a tenth of your spices — mint, dill and cumin. But you have neglected the more important matters of the law — justice, mercy and faithfulness" (Matthew 23:23). By narrowing the law to minor details, they had lost sight of its greater purpose.

In their obsession with religious control, the leaders had turned their traditions and temple power into idols. This broke the first commandment, for they worshiped status and authority rather than the living God, who now stood in their midst.

During His trial, further commandments were trampled. False witnesses stood before the council, directly violating the ninth commandment, "You shall not bear false witness" (Exodus 20:16; Deuteronomy 5:20; Matthew 19:18; Mark 10:19; Luke 18:20; James 2:11).

The leaders also misused the holy name of God, charging Jesus with blasphemy though He spoke the truth (Matthew 26:65). What should have been a pursuit of justice became an abuse of God's law.

This problem was not limited to ancient times; it remains a concern today. Even now, people can misuse free will by focusing on rules that make them look righteous while ignoring God's deeper call to love, compassion, and justice. Jesus' teaching reminds us that the law must be understood through the lens of God's character.

By fulfilling the law, Jesus also opened the way to freedom. The apostle Paul later wrote, "It is for freedom that Christ has set us free" (Galatians 5:1). This freedom is a release from the endless cycle of failure under the law. Because of Christ, believers are free to obey God out of love rather than fear.

Understanding the Bible Through Christ and the Law

Seeing how Jesus engaged the law helps us understand the Bible as one unified story. The commandments given at Sinai, the warnings of the prophets, and the teachings of Jesus all point to the same truth: God calls His people to love Him and live in obedience.

Free will makes this possible, but it also poses a constant danger of disobedience. Jesus came to write the law on human hearts, fulfilling Jeremiah's promise of a new covenant (Jeremiah 31:33).

The Cross: The Ultimate Act of Love

The ministry of Jesus led inevitably to the cross. His teaching confronted hypocrisy, His miracles drew crowds, and His claim to be the Son of God provoked opposition from the religious leaders and fear from the Roman rulers. Yet behind the human plotting was God's plan of redemption, foretold by the prophets and accomplished in Christ's willing sacrifice.

The commandments were broken even as the arrest unfolded. Judas traded loyalty for silver, echoing the warning against theft and greed (Matthew 26:15).

The leaders' cry, "We have no king but Caesar" (John 19:15), revealed their rejection of God's authority. In choosing human power over God's Son, they violated the very first commandment, placing another ruler in God's place.

The armed crowd came to seize an innocent man, already setting in motion the violation of the sixth commandment, "You shall not murder." Against these sins, Jesus stood firm, choosing obedience rather than retaliation.

Judas' betrayal was a violation of covenant loyalty. His unfaithfulness mirrored the spirit of adultery, breaking trust for selfish gain. Jesus remained the faithful Bridegroom, keeping covenant with His people even unto death.

Centuries earlier, Isaiah had written of a figure who would suffer for the sins of others: "He was pierced for our transgressions, he was crushed for our iniquities; the punishment that brought us peace was on him, and by his wounds we are healed" (Isaiah 53:5). Christians understand this prophecy as pointing directly to Jesus. The cross fulfilled God's purpose to rescue humanity from sin.

Jesus' death also reveals perfect obedience. On the night before His crucifixion, in the Garden of Gethsemane, He prayed, "Father, if you are willing, take this cup from me; yet not my will, but yours be done" (Luke 22:42).

Here, the tension of free will is most visible. Jesus, fully human, recoiled at the suffering ahead. Yet He freely chose to submit to the Father's will.

In that moment, Jesus demonstrated the heart of the tenth commandment, refusing to let wrongful desire overcome obedience.

Though His human nature wanted to avoid the coming suffering, He did not covet a different path or grasp at escape. Instead, He submitted to the Father's will, showing us how free will is rightly used in surrender to God.

This obedience, even to death on a cross, stood as the ultimate contrast to humanity's long history of disobedience (Philippians 2:8).

The cross is the clearest expression of God's love. "For God so loved the world that he gave his one and only Son" (John 3:16). Adam chose disobedience in the garden. Jesus chose obedience in another garden. Israel repeatedly broke the covenant. Jesus remained faithful. At Calvary, free will was used for surrender. Through His sacrifice, He bore the penalty of sin once for all (Hebrews 10:10).

Even in His final hours, Jesus embodied the commandments. On the cross, He honored His mother, entrusting her to the disciple John's care (John 19:26-27), keeping the fifth commandment to the very end. At the same time, the sixth commandment was violated as innocent blood was shed. Yet instead of condemning His executioners, He prayed, "Father, forgive them" (Luke 23:34). In His obedience and mercy, Jesus revealed the fullness of God's law.

The cross also answers the problem of the law. The commandments revealed God's standards, and no one could keep them perfectly. Sin demanded justice, and justice required a penalty. On the cross, Jesus took that penalty upon Himself. As Paul explained, Christ "redeemed us from the curse of the law by becoming a curse for us" (Galatians 3:13). The law was satisfied, opening the way for mercy.

Free Will at the Crossroads

The crucifixion confronted every witness with a choice. Some mocked, some wept, and some, like the Roman centurion, confessed, "Surely this man was the Son of God!" (Mark 15:39). That pattern continues today. The cross is a decision every person must face. God has acted in love, but He does not force obedience. Each individual must freely choose how to respond to Christ's sacrifice.

From the garden to Gethsemane, Jesus demonstrated what true obedience looks like. While others broke the commandments through greed, false witness, violence, and neglect, He fulfilled them perfectly. His faithfulness in the face of disobedience confirms that He is the true fulfillment of the law and the model for how free will can be used in harmony with God's will.

The Resurrection: Victory Over Sin and Death

If the story ended at the cross, it would be a tragedy. Jesus' death would stand as the martyrdom of a good teacher, another victim of injustice. Yet the Bible declares something greater: on the third day, the tomb was empty. The resurrection is the turning point of history, God's final word against sin and death.

On the first day of the week, women who had followed Jesus came to the tomb with spices to anoint His body. They found the stone rolled away and an angel who said, "Why do you look for the living among the dead? He is not here; he has risen!" (Luke 24:5-6). This moment confirmed that the cross was victorious. Death could not hold the Author of life (Acts 2:24).

Even in His burial, the Sabbath was honored. Jesus' body rested in the tomb on the seventh day, and His resurrection on the first day opened the way to the true Sabbath rest that Hebrews 4:9-10 promises for God's people.

The resurrection vindicated everything Jesus had said and done. He had claimed authority to forgive sins, to heal, and to judge, and the resurrection proved that His claims were true. Paul later wrote that Jesus "was declared with power to be the Son of God by his resurrection from the dead" (Romans 1:4). The resurrection was God's stamp of approval on Christ's mission.

The resurrection also accomplished what the law never achieved. Sin's penalty is death (Romans 6:23), yet Jesus broke the power of death by rising again. As Paul celebrated, "Death has been swallowed up in victory" (1 Corinthians 15:54). The curse of sin that had followed humanity from Adam was undone in Christ, the new Adam, who obeyed perfectly and opened the way to eternal life (1 Corinthians 15:22).

Even with the evidence of the empty tomb, the concept of free will remained central. Some, like the disciples, believed after seeing the risen Lord. Others, like the guards bribed to spread false reports (Matthew 28:11-15), rejected the truth. The resurrection demands a response. It is a historical fact and an invitation to faith. Each person must choose whether to accept the risen Christ as Lord or to turn away in unbelief.

Understanding the Bible without the resurrection is impossible. Every promise, every prophecy, and every law finds its fulfillment here. The story that began in Genesis with life given, lost through sin, and protected by law is completed in Christ's triumph over death. The resurrection assures believers that obedience is not in vain, that faith has a future, and that God's plan for humanity is life.

The New Covenant in Christ

The coming of Christ marks the culmination of the story of Scripture. From creation to covenant, from law to kingdom, the Bible shows the pattern of God's love and humanity's repeated disobedience. Free will was misused repeatedly, leading to brokenness, exile, and death. Yet God's plan was always to redeem His people. In Jesus, the plan reached its fulfillment.

Through His obedience, even to death on a cross, Christ accomplished what Adam, Israel, and every generation failed to do. He fulfilled the law perfectly, carried the penalty of sin, and opened the way to forgiveness. In His resurrection, He secured victory over death and offered new life to all who believe in Him. This is the new covenant Jeremiah had foretold: "I will put my law in their minds and write it on their hearts. I will be their God, and they will be my people" (Jeremiah 31:33).

This covenant rests on a living relationship with God through Christ. It is sealed with the blood of Jesus, shed once for all (Hebrews 9:12). It offers true freedom by breaking the power of sin and enabling obedience that flows from love.

Free will remains central in this covenant. God does not force anyone to believe. Just as Adam and Eve chose in Eden, and Israel chose in the wilderness, every person must now choose how to respond to Christ. The gift of salvation is offered freely, and it must be received by faith.

Understanding the Bible means seeing it as one continuous story that finds its climax in Christ. The promises, prophecies, and commandments all point to Him. The cross and the resurrection form the foundation for the rest of the story — the life of the church and the mission to bring God's love to the world.

Chapter 8

MODERN PARALLELS

The choices of free will did not end with Adam and Eve. They did not end with Cain, Noah, Abraham, or Israel. The same gift remains with us today.

God still shows us two sides. One side is how He wants us to live. The other side is how people actually live. Those sides are visible in the modern world just as clearly as they were in the ancient world.

We live in an age of speed and invention. Messages cross the world in seconds. Machines carry us over oceans in hours. Telescopes and satellites reveal parts of the universe that were previously invisible. These are wonders of human achievement. They are also tests of free will. The same gift that allowed Adam and Eve to choose still enables us to decide what to do with what we have been given.

Technology can serve God. A phone can display the Bible in many languages. A computer can disseminate sermons and worship songs. Screens can connect believers in prayer across great distances.

The gospel can now be preached to more people in one day than the apostles could have reached in a lifetime. Jesus told His disciples, "You will be my witnesses… to the ends of the earth" (Acts 1:8). Technology has made that possible in a way they could not have imagined.

The same devices can also become distractions. In restaurants and homes, people sit together but focus on their screens. In stadiums, crowds hold up phones to record what is already happening before their eyes. In churches, some heads are glued to glowing screens instead of bowing in prayer.

The tools are not inherently evil. The problem is how we choose to use them. Israel used gold to build the temple. They also used gold to make an idol. The metal was the same. The choice was different. In the same way, our devices can serve God, or they can serve our distractions. Free will decides the outcome.

Jesus said, "Where your treasure is, there your heart will be also" (Matthew 6:21). If our treasure is found in endless scrolling, in the pursuit of likes and followers, or in shallow amusement, then our hearts will be shaped by those things. If our treasure is found in God, then our hearts will be shaped by Him. Technology becomes a servant, not a master, when we use it to honor the Lord.

Money and Materialism

Jesus warned, "No one can serve two masters. Either you will hate the one and love the other... You cannot serve both God and money" (Matthew 6:24). That warning is as true now as it was two thousand years ago.

Money itself is not evil. It is a tool, like technology. It can provide food, clothing, shelter, and support for families. It can fund missions, care for the poor, and build churches. Yet when money becomes the center of life, it turns into an idol.

In the ancient world, people stored up grain, silver, and cattle to show their wealth. Today, we measure wealth in bank accounts, investments, and possessions.

The heart behind it is the same. People want more than they need. They choose comfort over contentment. They follow desire rather than God.

Debt reveals the extent to which the problem has escalated. Credit card bills pile up. Families borrow more than they can repay.

People buy new cars, furniture, and clothes not because they need them, but because they want them. Advertisements promise happiness in the next purchase, but the joy never lasts. The pattern only repeats. *"The eyes of man are never satisfied"* (Proverbs 27:20).

Jesus taught us to live by need, not by want. Needs are simple: food, clothing, shelter, and love. Wants multiply without end. The Israelites in the wilderness had manna each day, yet they complained because they wanted more. Today, we may have enough to live, yet we hunger for more. The human heart has not changed.

Free will is also at work here. Each person chooses how to view money. Some see it as a gift to be managed under God's direction. Others see it as a master to be served at any cost. Jesus told us plainly: we cannot serve both God and money. One will rule. One will guide the heart.

Abortion and the Value of Life

From the beginning, God gave three gifts to every human being: the breath of life, the soul, and free will. Life is His first gift. It begins at conception, when God breathes life into the body that He forms. The psalmist said, "You knit me together in my mother's womb" (Psalm 139:13). Life belongs to God, and it is holy.

Abortion denies this gift. It takes away life before it can grow. It rejects God's design and places human choice above His command. People say it is about freedom, but it is a freedom used against the very Author of life. This is the misuse of free will.

The Bible shows us God's care for the unborn. Jeremiah heard the Lord say, "Before I formed you in the womb I knew you" (Jeremiah 1:5). John the Baptist leapt in his mother's womb when Mary came near with the unborn Christ (Luke 1:41). These verses remind us that life in the womb is already life before God.

In ancient times, some nations sacrificed children to idols. God called it an abomination. He judged His people when they copied those practices. Today, abortion is defended with new words and modern arguments, but the act is the same. It is the destruction of life that God created.

Each culture must choose how it views life. Some honor it from the moment of conception. Others treat it as a matter of convenience. Free will again makes the difference. God has given us the choice, but He has also given us His clear word: "Choose life, that you and your children may live" (Deuteronomy 30:19).

Gender and Human Identity

When God created humanity, He made His design plain. *"So God created mankind in his own image, in the image of God he created them; male and female he created them"* (Genesis 1:27). Male and female were not accidents of biology but gifts of God's order. Together they reflect His image.

Today, many reject that order. Some claim that gender can be chosen or changed. Others teach that identity is self-defined, apart from the Creator. This is not new.

From the beginning, human beings have tried to rewrite God's word and redefine His design. Israel often twisted His commandments to suit their desires. Kings made their own laws and called them good. Prophets had to remind them that God's word does not change.

The same pattern repeats now. Instead of listening to the Creator, people listen to their own hearts. Yet Scripture warns, *"The heart is deceitful above all things and beyond cure. Who can understand it?"* (Jeremiah 17:9). The heart without God cannot guide us into truth. Only the One who made us can tell us who we are.

Jesus confirmed God's original design when He said, *"Haven't you read... that at the beginning the Creator 'made them male and female'"* (Matthew 19:4). He tied this truth to the union of marriage, showing that gender was part of God's plan for family, community, and holiness.

Free will allows each person to choose how to live with this truth. Some accept God's design and live in harmony with it. Others reject it and try to craft their own identity. The choice is real, but the outcome is also real. God's way leads to life and peace. Humanity's way leads to confusion and brokenness.

Sabbath and Worship

From the beginning, God set apart one day for rest and worship. *"By the seventh day God had finished the work he had been doing; so on the seventh day he rested from all his work. Then God blessed the seventh day and made it holy"* (Genesis 2:2-3). The Sabbath was not only about rest. It was about remembering the Creator and giving Him honor.

Israel often failed to keep the Sabbath. Prophets spoke against the people for treating it like any other day. Through Isaiah, God said, *"If you keep your feet from breaking the Sabbath and from doing as you please on my holy day… then you will find your joy in the Lord"* (Isaiah 58:13–14). The command was clear. The people chose otherwise.

The same pattern is visible today. Many set aside Sunday, even though it is not the seventh day. The Sabbath was always on Saturday, but some people, out of free will, changed it to Sunday in 325 A.D.

Even then, worship is often given little place in busy lives. Families plan outings, shopping, or entertainment first. Church becomes optional. If schedules allow, people attend. If not, God is set aside.

Jesus reminded His followers that the Sabbath was made for man, not man for the Sabbath (Mark 2:27). It was a gift, not a burden. A day to pause, to worship, to remember that life depends on God. Ignoring it shows how free will can be misused. We choose convenience over devotion. We honor our own time instead of God's time.

The call of the Sabbath is still the same. God's laws do not change. We can use our free will to honor Him with our time, or we can fill every hour with ourselves. One way leads to renewal. The other leads to emptiness.

The Narrow Road Today

Jesus told His disciples, *"Enter through the narrow gate. For wide is the gate and broad is the road that leads to destruction, and many enter through it. But small is the gate and narrow the road that leads to life, and only a few find it"* (Matthew 7:13-14). Those words explain our moment as much as they explained His.

The wide road is easily visible. It is filled with glowing screens, endless shopping, and lives lived for self. It is crowded with choices that deny God's gift of life, His design for humanity, and His command to worship. It is spacious, well-lit, and bustling with people.

The narrow road looks different. It is quieter. It calls for obedience when the world calls for freedom. It asks for humility when the world demands pride. It requires trust when the world urges control. Few choose it, but it is the road that leads to Christ.

Free will is at the center of this choice. God gave us the ability to decide how we will live. He has shown us His way through His Word and through His Son.

He has also allowed us to see what happens when people choose the other way. The Bible records both sides. History records both sides. Our world today shows both sides.

Every person stands at the same crossroad. The wide road promises ease, pleasure, and freedom. The narrow road offers truth, holiness, and life with God. The decision is ultimately up to each of us. But the outcome is eternal.

Chapter 9
REVELATION AND THE END
OF ALL THINGS

At the beginning of this book, we examined the three gifts God gives to every person: life, the soul, and free will. These gifts are not temporary. They remain with us until the end. They are the thread that runs through all of history. From Adam and Eve in the garden to John on the island of Patmos, the gifts of God have shaped every human story.

Revelation is the last book of the Bible. It is also the place where these gifts find their completion. Life, which began with God breathing into Adam, now reaches eternal life or eternal death.

The soul, which was given as a spark of God's image, now stands before Him in judgment. Free will, which once reached for forbidden fruit, now decides whether to worship the Lamb or the beast. The same gifts that were given in the beginning remain present at the end, but their weight is greater.

John, the disciple whom Jesus loved, wrote Revelation while exiled on the island of Patmos. He said, *"I, John, your brother and companion in the suffering and kingdom and patient endurance that are ours in Jesus, was on the island of Patmos because of the word of God and the testimony of Jesus"* (Revelation 1:9). Alone, banished, and facing the power of Rome, John was shown a vision that stretched from heaven to earth and from the present to the very end of time.

The first words of the book remind us what it is about: *"The revelation from Jesus Christ, which God gave him to show his servants what must soon take place"* (Revelation 1:1).

Revelation is not only a vision of judgment and symbols. It is the final unveiling of Jesus Christ. It shows Him as the beginning and the end, the Alpha and the Omega, the faithful witness, the ruler of the kings of the earth (Revelation 1:5, 8).

In the first chapters of this book, we saw how life and free will were given, and how quickly they were misused. Adam and Eve chose disobedience. Cain chose violence. Humanity began with gifts but turned them toward destruction.

Revelation brings the story full circle. It shows what happens when those same gifts are carried through all of history. The choices made by nations, churches, and individuals lead here to the throne of God, to the final judgment, to heaven or to hell.

The Bible begins with a garden. It ends with a city. In the garden, Adam and Eve walked with God, but they were driven out by sin. In the city, the redeemed walk with God forever, and no sin can drive them away.

In the garden, the tree of life was barred by an angel with a flaming sword (Genesis 3:24). In the city, the tree of life grows on both sides of the river of life, bearing fruit each month for the healing of the nations (Revelation 22:2). What was lost is restored. What was begun in creation is completed in the new creation.

This is the message of Revelation: God's way will prevail. The gifts He gave at the beginning are not wasted. They reach their final purpose in Christ. But the same choice still remains. Will we use life, soul, and free will to follow God's way? Or will we use them to follow the world's way? Revelation shows us the result of each path, not as theory, but as reality.

Christ Revealed as the Fulfillment of God's Way

At the center of Revelation is not a code, a beast, or a timeline. At the center is a person. John did not first see the end of the world. He first saw the risen Christ.

He wrote, *"I turned around to see the voice that was speaking to me. And when I turned, I saw seven golden lampstands, and among the lampstands was someone like a son of man, dressed in a robe reaching down to his feet and with a golden sash around his chest. The hair on his head was white like wool, as white as snow, and his eyes were like blazing fire. His feet were like bronze glowing in a furnace, and his voice was like the sound of rushing waters"* (Revelation 1:12-15).

This vision of Christ is unlike anything in the gospels. John had walked with Jesus. He had leaned on Him at the Last Supper. He had seen Him on the cross. But now he saw the Lord in glory. The carpenter from Nazareth was revealed as the King of kings and Lord of lords.

Jesus spoke to John and said, *"Do not be afraid. I am the First and the Last. I am the Living One; I was dead, and now look, I am alive for ever and ever! And I hold the keys of death and Hades"* (Revelation 1:17-18). These words show us the fulfillment of God's way. From the beginning, God gave life. Now Jesus declares that He is life itself. From the beginning, humanity feared death. Now Jesus declares that He holds the keys.

In Chapter 1 of this book, we considered the gifts of God: life, the soul, and free will. In Jesus, we see those gifts restored. He is life, given for the world. He is the one who redeems the soul from sin and death. He is the one who offers true freedom — not freedom to sin, but freedom from sin. Paul wrote, *"For as in Adam all die, so in Christ all will be made alive"* (1 Corinthians 15:22). Adam's failure is undone by Christ's victory.

Jesus is called the Alpha and the Omega, the first and the last (Revelation 22:13). Alpha is the first letter of the Greek alphabet. Omega is the last. He is the beginning and the end of history. Nothing starts without Him. Nothing ends apart from Him. Just as the gifts of God began in Him at creation, they are brought to completion in Him at the end.

This is why Revelation is not simply a book of doom. It is a book of hope. It not only shows the power of evil. It shows the greater power of Christ. John wrote, *"To him who loves us and has freed us from our sins by his blood… to him be glory and power for ever and ever! Amen"* (Revelation 1:5–6). That is the heart of Revelation. The same God who gave gifts in the beginning has now given His Son to bring those gifts to their true end.

When Adam sinned, the gifts of God were twisted. Life became subject to death. The soul became stained by sin. Free will became bent toward rebellion. But in Christ, those same gifts are redeemed. Life becomes eternal. The soul becomes purified. Free will becomes able to choose God's way through the Spirit. This is what Revelation shows us — the Lamb who was slain is also the King who reigns. He is both sacrifice and judge, both redeemer and ruler.

John fell at His feet "as though dead" (Revelation 1:17). That is the proper response. The vision of Christ is overwhelming. But the first words of Jesus to John are also the first words of the gospel: *"Do not be afraid."* The end is not meant to fill believers with fear but with faith. For those who belong to Christ, Revelation is not the story of loss. It is the story of final victory.

Humanity's Final Choices

From the beginning, human beings have faced a choice. Adam and Eve chose whether to trust God's command or reach for what He had forbidden. Cain chose whether to offer what God desired or to give what pleased himself. Each choice carried a consequence. In the end, Revelation shows that humanity is still choosing — but now the results are eternal.

John's vision makes the contrast clear. On one side stands the Lamb, who was slain but lives forever. On the other side stands the beast, who demands worship and deceives the nations. The question is simple: whom will humanity follow?

John saw the faithful gathered around the throne. *"After this, I looked, and there before me was a great multitude that no one could count, from every nation, tribe, people, and language, standing before the throne and before the Lamb. They were wearing white robes and were holding palm branches in their hands. And they cried out in a loud voice: 'Salvation belongs to our God, who sits on the throne, and to the Lamb'"* (Revelation 7:9–10). This is the picture of those who used free will to choose God's way. They trusted in Christ, and they now share in His victory.

But John also saw those who chose another way. He wrote, *"All inhabitants of the earth will worship the beast—all whose names have not been written in the Lamb's book of life"* (Revelation 13:8).

The same free will that could have led them to God instead led them away from Him. They gave their devotion to power, pride, and false gods. They repeated the choice of Cain, offering what was corrupt instead of what was holy.

In the early chapters of this book, we saw how small choices led to great consequences. A single act of disobedience in Eden brought death into the world.

A single act of envy in Cain's heart led to the first murder. In Revelation, those choices are magnified across nations and generations. Some choose the Lamb and find life. Others choose the beast and face destruction. The pattern has not changed.

The letters to the seven churches (Revelation 2–3) show this same choice on a smaller scale. Some churches remained faithful under persecution. Others compromised with the world. Jesus told the church in Smyrna, *"Be faithful, even to the point of death, and I will give you life as your victor's crown"* (Revelation 2:10).

But He warned the church in Laodicea, *"Because you are lukewarm—neither hot nor cold—I am about to spit you out of my mouth"* (Revelation 3:16). Even within the church, free will divides people into obedience and rebellion.

This is the reality Revelation places before us. Humanity has always had choices. In the end, those choices become clear. We either stand with the Lamb or we bow to the beast.

There is no middle ground. Just as Cain could not undo the consequence of his offering, and just as Adam and Eve could not remain in Eden after disobedience, so humanity cannot escape the results of its final choice.

Free will is both a gift and a test. In Revelation, the test is completed. Every person's choice is revealed. The faithful receive robes of white. The rebellious follow the beast into judgment. The line first drawn in Eden is finally completed in eternity.

Judgment as the Consequence of Choice

When Adam and Eve disobeyed, they were sent out of the garden. When Cain murdered his brother, he was marked and driven away from the land. Sin brought separation. Every choice against God carried a judgment. Revelation shows that this truth has not changed. The only difference is that judgment now comes on a global scale.

John saw the unfolding of God's judgment in a series of visions. He wrote of seven seals, seven trumpets, and seven bowls. Each one revealed what happens when the world chooses rebellion. *"Then I watched as the Lamb opened one of the seven seals, and I heard one of the four living creatures say in a voice like thunder, 'Come!' I looked, and there before me was a white horse! Its rider held a bow, and he was given a crown, and he rode out as a conqueror bent on conquest"* (Revelation 6:1–2). War, famine, disease, and death followed. Humanity chose pride and power, and the result was destruction.

The trumpets revealed further judgment. *"The first angel sounded his trumpet, and there came hail and fire mixed with blood, and it was hurled down on the earth. A third of the earth was burned up"* (Revelation 8:7). The bowls poured out even greater wrath, showing the full weight of sin against a holy God. These visions are not only future warnings.

They are echoes of the same pattern seen from the beginning: sin leads to judgment, rebellion leads to exile.

Just as Cain could not remain near his family after killing Abel, those who follow the beast cannot remain near God. Revelation 18 describes the fall of Babylon, a symbol of human pride and corruption: *"Fallen! Fallen is Babylon the Great! She has become a dwelling for demons and a haunt for every impure spirit"* (Revelation 18:2). The city that exalted itself against God collapses in ruin.

The final picture is the great white throne. *"Then I saw a great white throne and him who was seated on it. The earth and the heavens fled from his presence, and there was no place for them. And I saw the dead, great and small, standing before the throne, and books were opened. Another book was opened, which is the book of life. The dead were judged according to what they had done as recorded in the books"* (Revelation 20:11-12). At this moment, exile becomes eternal. Those who choose God's way are welcomed into His presence. Those who chose against Him are cast out forever.

Judgment is not God's delight, but it is His justice. Adam and Eve were warned before they sinned. Cain was warned before he struck his brother. In the same way, Revelation gives warning after warning. The seals, trumpets, and bowls are not only punishments — they are chances to repent. Yet John records, *"The rest of mankind who were not killed by these plagues still did not repent of the work of their hands"* (Revelation 9:20). Free will remains to the end, and many still choose rebellion.

Revelation reminds us that sin always separates. It separated Adam and Eve from the garden. It separated Cain from his family. And in the end, it separates humanity from God. The choices we make with the gifts He has given us lead either to His presence or to His judgment. The consequence of choice cannot be avoided.

Heaven vs. Hell — The Two Outcomes of Free Will

At the beginning of this book, we reflected on the gifts God gave to every person: life, the soul, and free will. Those gifts were meant for good. Yet from the start, they were misused. Adam and Eve chose disobedience. Cain chose hatred. The pattern continued through Israel's history and the church's failures. Revelation shows us where those choices finally lead. The gifts of God remain, but their outcomes are now eternal.

On one side stands heaven. John wrote, *"Then I saw a new heaven and a new earth, for the first heaven and the first earth had passed away... I saw the Holy City, the new Jerusalem, coming down out of heaven from God, prepared as a bride beautifully dressed for her husband"* (Revelation 21:1–2). In this city, God dwells with His people. *"He will wipe every tear from their eyes. There will be no more death or mourning or crying or pain, for the old order of things has passed away"* (Revelation 21:4). Life, the first gift, is now eternal and without sorrow.

The soul also finds its completion. *"They will see his face, and his name will be on their foreheads"* (Revelation 22:4). To see God's face is to know Him fully. The soul, made in His image, is restored to perfect fellowship. The exile that began in Eden is undone. The angel who once barred the tree of life now shows it open to all who belong to the Lamb: *"On each side of the river stood the tree of life, bearing twelve crops of fruit, yielding its fruit every month. And the leaves of the tree are for the healing of the nations"* (Revelation 22:2). What was lost is given again.

Free will also reaches its final purpose. Those who chose Christ now choose Him forever. Their decision is sealed, their worship unbroken. They cry out, *"Worthy is the Lamb, who was slain, to receive power and wealth and wisdom and strength and honor and glory and praise!"* (Revelation 5:12). Their free will, once able to rebel, is now perfectly united with God's will.

But on the other side stands hell. John wrote, *"Then death and Hades were thrown into the lake of fire. The lake of fire is the second death. Anyone whose name was not found written in the book of life was thrown into the lake of fire"* (Revelation 20:14-15). Here, the gifts are still present, but they are twisted. Life becomes eternal death. The soul becomes eternally separated from God. Free will becomes eternally fixed against Him.

Jesus described hell as a place *"where the worm does not die, and the fire is not quenched"* (Mark 9:48). It is not simply the absence of God's blessing. It is the presence of His judgment. Just as Cain bore a mark of separation, and Adam and Eve were barred from Eden, those who reject God now face a final and unending exile.

The difference between heaven and hell is not in God's gifts. Both groups received life, soul, and free will. The difference is in how those gifts were used. One group chose to worship God, and their gifts became eternal joy. The other chose to reject Him, and their gifts became eternal loss. Revelation does not soften this contrast. It makes it plain.

Heaven and hell are not accidents. They are the outcomes of choice. From the garden to the final throne, the story is the same. God gives. Humanity chooses. And in the end, the choice becomes eternal.

The Final Call to Choose

The Bible does not end with silence. It ends with a call. John wrote, *"The Spirit and the bride say, 'Come!' And let the one who hears say, 'Come!' Let the one who is thirsty come; and let the one who wishes take the free gift of the water of life"* (Revelation 22:17). After visions of judgment and glory, heaven and hell, this is the final invitation.

It takes us back to the first gift of free will. God does not force anyone into heaven, and He does not push anyone into hell. He gives life, He gives the soul, He gives free will — and then He calls. Each person must decide. The choice is not hidden. It is plain. Come to Christ and live. Turn away and face the second death.

The final words of Revelation echo the urgency of the moment: *"Yes, I am coming soon."* Amen. Come, Lord Jesus (Revelation 22:20). Christ's return is not far off in some distant future. It is always near.

Every generation is called to live as if He may return today. Every heart is called to be ready.

This is where the gifts of God find their end. Life becomes eternal life or eternal death. The soul enters God's presence or is shut out forever. Free will is sealed either in worship or in rebellion. The coin first placed in Adam's hand is now laid before the throne. On one side is the face of God, shining forever. On the other side is the face of sin, turned away from Him for eternity.

The road is still narrow. Jesus said, *"Enter through the narrow gate... small is the gate and narrow the road that leads to life, and only a few find it"* (Matthew 7:13-14). Revelation shows what happens when that road comes to its end. The wide road leads to destruction. The narrow road leads to the Lamb, to the city of God, to the tree of life.

The choice belongs to every soul. It began in the garden. It continues in every generation. And it will be revealed in eternity. The Spirit still says, "Come." The church still says, "Come." And those who are thirsty still hear the voice of Christ: *"Let anyone who is thirsty come to me and drink"* (John 7:37). The final page of Scripture leaves us with this truth: God calls, and we must choose.

Chapter 10

CHOOSING THE WAY

Every human being carries a coin in the pocket of their soul. On one side is life with God. On the other side is life without Him.

The coin itself is the same for everyone — it is the gift of free will. From the richest king to the poorest beggar, from the scientist studying galaxies to the child learning to read, each one has this coin.

Joshua knew this when he gathered Israel at Shechem. The people had crossed rivers, fought battles, and inherited land. They had seen the power of God with their eyes. Yet Joshua stood before them and said, *"Choose for yourselves this day whom you will serve"* (Joshua 24:15). He did not ask about yesterday's victories or tomorrow's plans. He asked about today's decision. The coin was in their hand, and he demanded they turn it one way or the other.

We live with the same coin. Every morning, we flip it, though not always with thought. We choose whether our words will bless or wound. We choose whether our work will honor God or honor ourselves. We choose whether to forgive or to hold on to bitterness. These small turns of the coin shape the direction of our lives. They are like footsteps on a long road. One step may seem small, but over time, it sets the path of an entire journey.

Paul warned the Galatians, *"A man reaps what he sows"* (Galatians 6:7). Farmers understand this truth. They do not expect wheat from seeds of thorns, or grapes from seeds of weeds. The field produces according to what was planted. Our lives do the same. Each choice plants something in the soil of eternity. At first glance, the field appears bare. But in time, the harvest reveals what kind of seed was sown.

Jesus put it in sharper terms: *"Whoever is not with me is against me"* (Matthew 12:30). There is no middle ground. It must land on one face or the other. That is why free will is such a heavy gift. It feels light in the hand, but it carries the weight of eternity.

This is where all of Scripture leads us. In the garden, Adam and Eve turned their backs on God. In the wilderness, Israel often did the same. In Revelation, John saw the outcome of such choices written across nations and empires. But the final question is not about them. It is about us. The coin is in your hand and mine. Which way will it fall?

The Weight of Free Will

Free will may seem insignificant, but it is never trivial. It is like a set of scales we carry with us everywhere. Every word, every habit, every desire places weight on one side or the other. Over time, the scales tip, and the direction of the soul becomes clear.

The writer of Proverbs warned, *"There is a way that appears to be right, but in the end it leads to death"* (Proverbs 14:12). That single verse captures the weight of free will. The path that feels natural, easy, or popular may seem harmless at first. Yet one decision becomes two, and two becomes a pattern, and the pattern becomes a destiny. What looked right in the moment ends in ruin.

Paul described this same truth in the language of the Spirit and the flesh. *"The acts of the flesh are obvious: sexual immorality, impurity and debauchery; idolatry and witchcraft; hatred, discord, jealousy, fits of rage, selfish ambition, dissensions, factions and envy"* (Galatians 5:19-21).

None of these choices may seem final on their own. A moment of anger. A flash of envy. A careless indulgence. Yet together they form a road, and Paul warns that this road leads to exclusion from the kingdom of God.

In contrast, the fruit of the Spirit grows where free will bends toward God: *"love, joy, peace, forbearance, kindness, goodness, faithfulness, gentleness and self-control"* (Galatians 5:22-23).

These too are choices, made day after day. A kind word instead of a sharp reply. A moment of patience instead of a burst of frustration. A prayer lifted instead of a complaint spoken. Over time, the field of a person's life begins to show what was sown.

Think of a river splitting into two streams. Initially, the water originates from the same source. The streams run side by side, and at first the distance between them is narrow. But the further they run, the wider the gap grows.

One stream may lead to fertile valleys, the other to dry wastelands. Free will is like that fork in the river. A single turn sets the direction, and the longer the flow continues, the more difficult it becomes to reverse.

Modern life provides numerous examples of how free will holds significance. A worker chooses to shade the truth on a report, thinking it will protect him for a day.

A student cheats on one exam, certain it will never matter again. A husband or wife nurses a quiet resentment, refusing to forgive. These choices may seem hidden, but they carve channels in the soul. Over the years, those channels have determined whether water flows toward life or toward decay.

Jesus told a parable about two people building a house. One built his house on a rock. The other was built on sand. Both houses stood for a time. Both seemed secure. However, when the storm arrived, the difference was revealed. *"The rain came down, the streams rose, and the winds blew and beat against that house, and it fell with a great crash"* (Matthew 7:27). Free will is the daily decision of where to lay the next stone: rock or sand. One choice may not look decisive. But the house will reveal what foundation was chosen.

The weight of free will is that no choice is ever neutral. Every step moves us closer to God or further away. Every seed grows into a harvest. Every stone becomes part of a house. Free will is the gift we all share, but it is also the burden we all carry. And in the end, those choices are not temporary. They become eternal.

The Two Roads

Life often feels like a tangle of paths, twisting in every direction. Choices crowd us, decisions press on us, and the future seems uncertain. Yet Jesus simplified the matter with a startling image. He said, *"Enter through the narrow gate. For wide is the gate and broad is the road that leads to destruction, and many enter through it. But small is the gate and narrow the road that leads to life, and only a few find it"* (Matthew 7:13-14). According to Him, there are not a hundred paths in the end. There are only two.

Rev. Billy Graham, one of the most well-known Christian preachers of the twentieth century, often spoke about this very choice. He traveled the world for more than fifty years, preaching to millions, and his central message was always the same: every person must decide for Christ. Graham described life as standing at the edge of two highways. One is wide, smooth, and crowded.

The other is narrow, steep, and lonely. From a distance, the wide road looks appealing. It is filled with noise, laughter, and movement. People rush forward without much thought, swept along by the current. The narrow road looks harder. Few people walk it. The way is tight, and the climb is steep. But at the end of each road stands a destination. The wide road ends in destruction. The narrow road ends in life.

Imagine standing on an overpass above a great highway. Below you, cars stream endlessly, headlights stretching into the horizon. The flow is constant, relentless, and fast. That is the wide road of life — crowded, bright, and filled with confidence. But at the horizon, where the road disappears, smoke rises. The journey that looked so exciting leads only to ruin.

Now, picture a small trail cutting away from the highway. It winds upward through rocky ground. It is not well-lit, and only a few travelers take it. Their pace is slower. Their burdens are heavier. From the highway, the trail looks foolish. Yet at the top of the ridge, where the path ends, there is light. A city gleams, and its gates are open. That is the narrow road of life. Hard in the walking, but glorious in its ending.

The two roads are not marked by signs of stone but by habits of the heart. The wide road is paved with selfishness, pride, and distraction. People travel it when they choose to serve themselves, to chase pleasure, to worship idols of success or comfort. It feels wide because anything seems to fit. Every desire is welcomed. Every indulgence is permitted. But the pavement cracks beneath the weight of sin, and the road cannot hold.

The narrow road is different. It is not wide enough for a pride to pass through. It does not allow us to carry every possession or ambition. To walk it, we must lay things down. Jesus said, *"Whoever wants to be my disciple must deny themselves and take up their cross daily and follow me"* (Luke 9:23). That is the narrowness of the path. It requires surrender. But in surrender, there is freedom. The weight that once bent our backs is left behind, and the climb, though steep, leads upward.

Every day, we place our feet on one of these two roads. Choosing the wide road does not always look dramatic. It may look like indifference, ignoring God while moving with the crowd. It may look like comfort, seeking only ease and pleasure. It may look like a compromise, blending in with whatever culture demands. But each step leads closer to the horizon of destruction.

Choosing the narrow road may not look dramatic either. It may look like a quiet prayer before work. A refusal to join in gossip. A decision to forgive. A sacrifice made in secret. Yet each step presses the soul upward toward life. The road is not wide, but it is true. The company is not large, but it is faithful. The destination is not temporary, but eternal.

Jesus gave the image of the two roads to show us that free will is never without direction. We are always walking, always moving. The only question is which road our steps are on. Billy Graham often ended his sermons with a call to choose. He would remind his listeners that crowds on the wide road cannot carry them to safety. Salvation is personal. The narrow road must be chosen one soul at a time.

Standing at the crossroads, the choice seems simple. Yet it is the most serious choice we will ever face. For at the end of the wide road stands destruction, and at the end of the narrow road stands Christ.

Heaven or Hell: The Final Destination

Every journey reaches its end. The Bible does not allow us to imagine that life drifts into a vague afterthought. The paths we walk, the choices we make, and the road we follow all lead to a final destination. Jesus described it with stark clarity in the parable of the sheep and the goats: *"Then they will go away to eternal punishment, but the righteous to eternal life"* (Matthew 25:46). Two outcomes. No middle ground.

Heaven is not merely a place of reward. It is the presence of God Himself. John's vision speaks of a city where *"the Lord God Almighty and the Lamb are its temple"* (Revelation 21:22). No temple is needed because God is everywhere present. No sun or lamp is needed because *"the glory of God gives it light, and the Lamb is its lamp"* (Revelation 21:23). The essence of heaven is not golden streets or pearly gates. It is unhindered communion with the One who made us.

Hell, by contrast, is not merely punishment. It is a separation from that presence. Jesus called it *"outer darkness,"* where there is *"weeping and gnashing of teeth"* (Matthew 8:12). It is a place where desire continues but satisfaction never comes, where memory lingers but hope does not. The torment of hell is not only what is present — fire, thirst, and judgment — but what is absent: the love of God, the joy of fellowship, the rest of the soul.

What makes this destination so sobering is that it flows directly from the daily exercise of free will. Paul warned in Romans, *"To those who by persistence in doing good seek glory, honor and immortality, he will give eternal life. But for those who are self-seeking and who reject the truth and follow evil, there will be wrath and anger"* (Romans 2:7-8). Heaven and hell are not arbitrary assignments. They are the ripened fruit of the seeds sown in life.

Consider a tree. Two saplings may look alike when they are young. Their leaves are green, their branches thin, their roots shallow. But give them years, and their true nature emerges. One bears good fruit. The other bears thorns. Jesus said, *"By their fruit you will recognize them"* (Matthew 7:20). In the same way, the final judgment does not invent our destiny. It reveals what has already been growing in us.

This is why the call of Scripture is so urgent. Every step on the wide road or the narrow road is shaping the soul toward its eternal end. Every decision with the coin of free will is pressing the imprint of eternity deeper into us. The haunting truth is that hell is simply the wide road continued without end, while heaven is the narrow road opened into glory.

The final destination is not far off in a distant land. It is the horizon toward which we are already walking. The road beneath our feet today is the road that will carry us there tomorrow. The question is not whether we will arrive at an end. The question is only where.

Choose Today

At the end of his life, Joshua gathered Israel and drew a line in the sand: *"Choose for yourselves this day whom you will serve"* (Joshua 24:15). His challenge was not for tomorrow or for when life became easier. It was for that very moment. The same call comes to us now. We cannot postpone it forever. To delay is, in itself, a choice.

The coin of free will still rests in every hand. From the beginning of this book, we have traced its weight through creation, covenant, prophets, Christ, the church, and Revelation's vision of the end. At last, it comes down to this: which side of the coin will remain when it lands? One side bears the face of Christ and the life He offers. The other side bears the imprint of sin and the death it demands. No one else can flip that coin for us.

Jesus warned that the gate is narrow and the way is hard, but it leads to life. He also promised, *"Whoever hears my word and believes him who sent me has eternal life and will not be judged but has crossed over from death to life"* (John 5:24). The choice is not about earning heaven through effort. It is about trusting the One who already bore our judgment and opened the road for us.

We are standing at the crossroads even now. On one side is the wide road, filled with noise, distraction, and self-assurance, leading only to destruction. On the other side is the narrow road, marked by surrender, faith, and obedience, leading to the Lamb and the city of God. The decision belongs to each soul.

The haunting image of Johnny Cash's *"Ghost Riders in the Sky"* lingers here. Riders chasing what they can never catch, trapped in the futility of wasted choices. Their warning echoes to us: "Change your ways before it is too late." Yet the voice of Scripture speaks louder: *"The Spirit and the bride say, 'Come!' And let the one who hears say, 'Come!' Let the one who is thirsty come; and let the one who wishes take the free gift of the water of life"* (Revelation 22:17).

Free will is a gift, but it is also a summons. The decision cannot be escaped. Every step is either toward life or toward death, toward heaven or toward hell. The coin must fall. The road must be chosen. And the time is now.

OVER TO YOU

When this book began, I admitted my own struggle with reading the Bible. Its stories felt scattered. Its laws felt heavy. Its message seemed hard to follow. For years, I carried questions: How do these ancient words fit together? What do they have to do with my life now? Perhaps you have felt the same.

Over time, I discovered a thread. From the first pages of Genesis to the last vision of Revelation, the Bible tells a single story. God gives His gifts—life, the soul, free will. Humanity responds—sometimes in obedience, often in rebellion. The outcome of those choices unfolds across history until the final invitation is spoken: "Let the one who is thirsty come" (Revelation 22:17).

Seeing this thread did not answer every question, yet it gave me clarity. The Bible speaks about choices made long ago and about the choices we face today. That is what makes it a living book. It speaks across centuries and also to this very moment.

If you have struggled, as I once did, to read and understand the Bible, I invite you to take it up again. Read it as a single story of God's gifts and human response. Read it with an ear for the invitation that runs throughout its pages: to choose life, to choose Christ, to choose the way that leads to God.

The Bible ends with hope and with a call. It leaves us with this truth: the story is not finished on the page. It continues in your life. Your free will, your choices, your response—these are now part of the story God is telling.

To understand the Bible is to enter it. And the invitation remains open: Come.